ALSO BY ROBERTO CALASSO

I. The Ruin of Kasch

II. The Marriage of Cadmus and Harmony

III. Ka

IV. K.

V. Tiepolo Pink

VI. La Folie Baudelaire

VII. Ardor

The Forty-nine Steps

Literature and the Gods

THE ART
OF THE PUBLISHER

THE ART
OF THE PUBLISHER

ROBERTO CALASSO

TRANSLATED FROM THE ITALIAN

BY RICHARD DIXON

FARRAR, STRAUS AND GIROUX

NEW YORK

Farrar, Straus and Giroux
18 West 18th Street, New York 10011

Originally published in Italian in 2013 by Adelphi Edizioni,
Italy, as *L'impronta dell'editore*
English translation published in the United States
by Farrar, Straus and Giroux
First American edition, 2015

Library of Congress Cataloging-in-Publication Data
Calasso, Roberto.
    [Impronta dell'editore. English]
    The art of the publisher / Roberto Calasso ; translated by
Richard Dixon.
        pages   cm
    ISBN 978-0-374-18823-8 (hardback) —ISBN 978-0-374-71183-2
(e-book)
    1. Publishers and publishing. 2. Publishers and publishing—
History. 3. Adelphi (Firm)—History. 4. Calasso, Roberto—
Career in publishing. 5. Publishers and publishing—
Biography.   I. Dixon, Richard, translator.   II. Title.

Z278.C2813 2015
070.5—dc23

                                              2015010108

Designed by Jonathan D. Lippincott

Contents

I
Publishing as a Literary Genre   3

II
Singular Books   17
A Letter to a Stranger   80

III
Giulio Einaudi   89
Luciano Foà   99
Roger Straus   104
Peter Suhrkamp   107
Vladimir Dimitrijević   111

IV
Faire Plaisir   119
The Obliteration of Publisher Identity   125
Aldus Manutius's Fly Sheet   132

Textual Note   147

I

PUBLISHING AS
A LITERARY GENRE

I'd like to address something that is generally taken for granted, but turns out not to be so obvious: the art of publishing books. And first of all I would like to consider the notion of publishing itself, for it seems to be shrouded by a number of misunderstandings. If someone is asked what a publishing house does, the general and most reasonable answer is the following: it is a lesser branch of industry that tries to make money publishing books. And what should a *good* publishing house be? We suppose a good publishing house to be one—if you'll allow the tautology—that publishes, so far as possible, *only* good books. Thus, to use a summary definition, those books of which the publisher tends to feel proud rather than ashamed. From this point of view, a good publishing house is unlikely to be of any particular interest in economic terms. Publishing good books has never made anyone terribly rich. Or, at least, not in comparison with what someone might make supplying the market with mineral water or microchips or buttons. It would appear that a publishing business can produce substantial profits only on condition that good books are submerged beneath many other things of very different quality. And when you are submerged, it is much easier to drown—and so disappear altogether.

It is also worth remembering that publishing has often shown itself to be a sure and rapid way of squandering substantial amounts of money. One might even add that, along with roulette and *cocottes*, founding a publishing house has always been one of the most effective ways for a young man of noble birth to fritter away his fortune. If this is so, we might wonder why the role of the publisher has attracted so many people over the centuries—and continues to be regarded as fascinating, and in some ways mysterious, even today. For example, it is not hard to see that no job title is more coveted by certain tycoons, who often obtain it literally at a high price. If such people were able to declare that they *publish* frozen vegetables, rather than produce them, they would presumably be very happy about it. We can therefore conclude that, apart from being one branch of business, publishing has always involved prestige, if only because it is a kind of business that is also an art. An art in every sense, and certainly a dangerous art since, in order to practice it, money is an essential element. From this point of view it can be argued that very little has changed since Gutenberg's time.

And yet, if we look back over five centuries of publishing and try to think of publishing as an art, we immediately see paradoxes of every kind. The first might be this: on the basis of what criteria can the greatness of a publisher be judged? On this point, as a Spanish friend of mine often used to say, there is no bibliography. We can read many learned and detailed studies of the work of certain publishers, but rarely do we come across any judgment about their greatness, as normally happens when dealing with writers or painters. So what goes into making a publisher great? A few examples: the first, and perhaps the most eloquent, takes us back to the origins of publishing. A phenomenon occurred in printing that would later be repeated with the birth of photography. It seems that we were introduced to these inventions by masters who immediately achieved an incomparable excellence. To understand what is essential about photography, all you have to do is study the work of Nadar. To understand what a great publishing house can be, all you have to do is look at the books printed by Aldus Manutius. He was the Nadar of publishing. He was the first to imagine a publishing house in terms of *form*. And here the word *form* has to be interpreted in many different ways. Form is crucial, first of all, in the choice and sequence of titles to be published. But form also relates to the texts that accompany the books, as well as the way in which the books are presented as objects. It therefore includes covers, graphics, layout, typeface, paper. It was usually Aldus himself who wrote those short

introductory texts—in the form of letters or *epistulae*—
that are the precursors not only of all modern introductions, prefaces, and afterwords, but also of all cover flaps,
catalogs, and publicity material of today. That was the
first indication that all books published by a certain
publisher could be seen as links in a single chain, or
segments in a serpentine progression of books, or fragments in a single book formed by all the books published by that publisher. This, obviously, is the most
hazardous and ambitious goal for a publisher, and so it
has remained for five hundred years. And if you think
that this is an unworkable enterprise, you may remember that literature loses all of its magic unless there's
an element of impossibility concealed deep within it.
I believe that something similar can be said about
publishing, or at least this particular way of being a
publisher—a way that has not been practiced very often
over the course of the centuries, but has sometimes produced memorable results. To give a sense of what can
emerge from this conception of publishing, I will describe two books published by Aldus Manutius. The first
was published in 1499 with the abstruse title *Hypnerotomachia Poliphili*, "The Strife of Love in a Dream."
Today it would be called a "first novel." Moreover one
by an unidentified author (and still an enigma), written in a sort of imaginary language, a sort of *Finnegans
Wake* consisting entirely of a mishmash of Italian,
Latin, and Greek (while Hebrew and Arabic appeared
in the woodcuts). A fairly risky operation, you might say.
But what did the book look like? It was a folio edition,

illustrated with magnificent woodcuts that provided a perfect visual accompaniment to the text—something even more risky. But at this point we have to add something else: the vast majority of bibliophiles regard it as the *most* beautiful book ever printed. And you can see this for yourself if you ever happen to come across a copy of the book, or even just a good facsimile. It was obviously a single, unrepeatable stroke of genius. And in creating it the publisher played a fundamental part. But you mustn't imagine that Manutius was great only as a provider of treasures for bibliophiles of future centuries. The second example that relates to him goes in a totally different direction. In 1501 and 1502, with his Virgil and Sophocles, Manutius invented "libelli portatiles in formam enchiridii" ("books that can be held in the hand"), otherwise described by him as "parva forma." Anyone fortunate enough to handle one of them today would immediately realize that they are the first pocket-sized books in history, the first paperbacks. By inventing such a book, Manutius transformed the way in which people read. The very act of reading thus radically changed. Looking at the title page, we can admire the elegance of the Greek italic typeface used here for the first time and which would later become an invaluable point of reference. Manutius therefore managed to achieve two opposite results: first to create a book such as the *Hypnerotomachia Poliphili* that would remain unequaled, and is virtually the archetype of a book that is one of a kind. Then, to create completely different books that would be copied millions and millions of times over, right up until today.

You may say, fine, this is all very interesting and relevant to the glories of the Italian Renaissance, but what does it have to do with us, and with publishers today, who are inundated by a growing mass of tablets, e-books, and DVDs—not to mention the various incestuous alliances between all these devices? In order to answer this question I'll give a few more examples. If I told you in no uncertain terms that in my view a good publisher today ought simply to try to do what Manutius did in Venice a year before the start of the sixteenth century, you might think I'm joking—but I'm not. And so I'll tell you about a twentieth-century publisher and show you how he worked in exactly that way, even though the circumstances were completely different. His name was Kurt Wolff. He was a young German, elegant, wealthy, though not excessively so. He wanted to publish new writers of high literary quality. And so he invented a series of short books, in an unusual format, called Der Jüngste Tag, "Judgment Day," a title that today seems highly appropriate for a series of books that mostly appeared in Germany during the First World War. If you look at these books, which are black in color, slim and austere, with labels glued on like school exercise books, you may find yourself thinking: "This is how a book by Kafka ought to be presented." And several of Kafka's stories were in fact published in this series. These included *The Metamorphosis*, in 1915, with a fine blue label and a black border. Kafka was a young, little-known, and extremely self-effacing writer at the time. But, reading the letters Kurt Wolff wrote to him, you are immediately aware, from his exquisite tact and gentle concern, that the publisher simply *knew* who his correspondent was.

Kafka wasn't the only young writer published by Kurt Wolff. In 1917, a fairly turbulent year for publishing, Kurt Wolff collected the writings of several young authors into a yearly almanac entitled *Vom jüngsten Tag*. Here are some of the authors in the almanac: Franz Blei, Albert Ehrenstein, Georg Heym, Franz Kafka, Else Lasker-Schüler, Carl Sternheim, Georg Trakl, Robert Walser. They are the names of young writers who found themselves together that year under the roof of the same young publisher. And those same names, without exception, are on the list of essential authors to be read by any young person of today wanting to discover German literature in the early years of the twentieth century.

At this point my argument ought to seem fairly clear. Aldus Manutius and Kurt Wolff, living four hundred years apart, each did nothing substantially different from the other. Indeed they were practicing the same *art of publishing*—though this art may go unnoticed by most people, including publishers. And this art can be judged in both cases by the same criteria, the first and last of which is *form*: the capacity to give form to a plurality of books as though they were the chapters of a single book. And all this while taking care—a passionate and obsessive care—over the appearance of every volume, over the way in which it is presented. And finally—and this is certainly a point of no small importance—taking care of how that book might be sold to the largest number of readers.

Around fifty years ago Claude Lévi-Strauss suggested we should regard one of the fundamental activities of mankind—namely the elaboration of myths—as a particular form of bricolage. After all, myths are constructed from ready-made elements, many deriving from other myths. At this point I respectfully suggest we should also consider the art of publishing as a form of bricolage. Try to imagine a publishing house as a single text formed not just by the totality of books that have been published there, but also by all its other constituent elements, such as the front covers, cover flaps, publicity, the quantity of copies printed and sold, or the different editions in which the same text has been presented. Imagine a publishing house in this way and you will find yourself immersed in a very peculiar landscape, something that you might regard as a literary work in itself, belonging to a genre all its own. A genre that can claim to have its own modern classics: for example, the vast domains of Gallimard, which extend from the dark forests and swamps of the Série noire to the plateaus of the Pléiade, though also including various pretty provincial cities or tourist resorts resembling the papier-mâché Potemkin villages, erected, in this case, not for a visit by Catherine the Great but for a season of literary prizes. And we well know that, when a publishing house expands in this way, it can assume a certain imperial character. And so the name Gallimard rings out as far as the remotest confines of the French language. Or, on another side, we might find ourselves in the vast properties of the Insel Verlag, which appear to have been owned for many years by an enlightened feudal lord who has at last bequeathed his estates to his most loyal and trusted stewards . . . I don't want to go any further, but already you can see how intricate maps can be devised in this manner.

By looking at publishing houses in this way, one of the more mysterious aspects of our profession might perhaps become clearer: why does a publisher reject a particular book? Because he realizes that publishing it would be like putting the wrong character into a novel, a figure who might throw the whole thing off balance or radically change it. A second point relates to money and copies: following this line we are forced to consider the idea that the capacity to make people read (or at least *buy*) certain books is a key factor in the quality of a publishing house. The market—or the relationship with that unknown, obscure being known as *the public*—is the first ordeal of the publisher, in the medieval sense of the word: a test of fire that can send a considerable amount of money up in smoke. Publishing could thus be described as a hybrid multimedia literary genre. And hybrid it certainly is. As for it becoming mixed up with other media, this fact is now obvious. But publishing, as a game, is nevertheless fundamentally the same as the old one played by Aldus Manutius. And a new author whom we come across with an obscure book is very much the same for us as the still elusive author of the book called *Hypnerotomachia Poliphili*. So long as the game lasts, I am sure there will always be someone ready to play it with passion. But if the rules should one day radically change, as we are sometimes led to fear, I am also equally sure we'll be able to turn our hand to some other activity—and we might instead find ourselves meeting up around a roulette or *écarté* or blackjack table.

I would like to end with a question and a paradox. To what extreme can the art of publishing be taken? Can it still be imagined in circumstances where certain essential conditions, such as money and the marketplace, basically disappear? The answer—surprisingly—is yes. At least if we look at an example that has come to us from Russia. At the height of the October Revolution, in those days that were, in the words of Alexander Blok, "a mix of anxiety, horror, penance, hope," when printing presses had already been indefinitely shut down and inflation was pushing up prices hour by hour, a group of writers—including the poet Vladislav Khodasevich, the thinker Nikolai Berdyaev, and the novelist Mikhail Osorgin, who then recorded those events—decided to throw themselves into the wild business of opening a Writers' Bookshop that would still enable books—and, above all, certain books—to circulate. The Writers' Bookshop soon became, in Osorgin's words, "the only bookshop in Moscow and in the whole of Russia where the first to arrive could buy a book 'without authorization.'"

What Osorgin and his friends had wanted to create was a small publishing company. But the situation made it impossible. And so they used the Writers' Bookshop as a sort of double for a publishing house. No longer a place that produced new books, but one that sought to house and circulate large numbers of books (some valuable, some ordinary, often incomplete, but all destined to oblivion) that had ended up at their shop stall through the wreck of history. It was important to keep certain practices alive: to continue to handle those rectangular paper objects, to leaf through them, order them, discuss them, read them in the pauses between one task and another, and finally to pass them on to other people. The important thing was to create and maintain an order, a form: reduced to its lowest and most basic definition, this is the very art of publishing. And this was how it was practiced in the Writers' Bookshop in Moscow between 1918 and 1922. It reached the acme of its noble history when the founders of the bookshop decided, as printed publishing was impracticable, to set about publishing a series of works with one single handwritten copy. The complete catalog of these books, which were literally one of a kind, remained in Osorgin's house in Moscow and was eventually lost. But, as a hovering phantom, it is still the model and the guiding star for anyone who attempts to become a publisher in hard times. And times are always hard.

II

SINGULAR BOOKS

In the beginning we spoke of *singular books*. Adelphi had not yet found a name for itself. Only a few things were certain: the critical edition of Nietzsche was enough to give direction to everything else. And then a series of classics, an ambitious project that sought to do well what had previously been done less well, and to do for the first time what had previously been disregarded. They were to be printed by Mardersteig, along with the Nietzsche edition. At the time it seemed normal, almost obligatory. Today it would be inconceivable (costs multiplied tenfold, et cetera). We liked the idea of these books being entrusted to the last of the great classic printers. But we liked even more the fact that this master printer had long worked with Kurt Wolff, Kafka's publisher.

For Roberto Bazlen, who had a swiftness of mind I have never since encountered, the critical edition of Nietzsche seemed almost obvious. Where else could we have started? Italy was still dominated by a culture where the epithet *irrational* implied the severest condemnation. The begetter of all things *irrational* could only be Nietzsche. In any event, that odd word, unhelpful to thought, became a label that covered virtually everything. And it also included a vast part of what was essential—which had often still not been published in Italy, largely due to that damning label.

In literature, the *irrational* was fondly linked to the *decadent*, another word of outright condemnation. Not just certain authors but certain genres were condemned in principle. Now, several decades later, it may seem amusing and hard to believe, but anyone with a good memory will remember that fantastic literature as a genre was considered murky and suspect. From this it can already be seen how the idea of publishing a novel such as Alfred Kubin's *The Other Side*, an example of fantastic literature in its purest state, as volume no. 1 in the Biblioteca Adelphi series, might appear provocative. Made so much worse by the proximity, at no. 3 in the series, of another fantastic novel: *The Manuscript Found in Saragossa* by Jan Potocki (and it didn't matter that this was a book that, by then, could have been considered a classic).

When Bazlen talked to me for the first time about the new publishing house that would become Adelphi— I can give the exact date and the place, since it was my twenty-first birthday, in May 1962, at the villa of Ernst Bernhard at Bracciano, where Bazlen and Ljuba Blumenthal (the Ljuba of the famous poem by Montale) were staying as guests for a few days—he naturally spoke at once about the critical edition of Nietzsche and the future series of classics. He was very happy about both, but what mattered most to him were the other books that the new publishing house would produce: those that Bazlen had come across at different times over the years and had never managed to get *passed* by the various Italian publishers with whom he had worked, including Bompiani and Einaudi. What were they? Strictly speaking, they could be anything: a Tibetan classic (the life of Milarepa) or an unknown English author of a single book (Christopher Burney) or the most popular introduction to that new branch of science which was ethology (*King Solomon's Ring* by Konrad Lorenz) or several fourteenth- and fifteenth-century treatises on Noh theater. These were the names that Bazlen gave for some of the first *books to be done*. What bound them together? This wasn't entirely clear. It was then that Bazlen, by way of explanation, began talking about *singular books*.

What is a *singular book*? The most eloquent example, once again, is volume no. 1 in the Biblioteca series: Alfred Kubin's *The Other Side*. It is a singular novel by a nonnovelist, in which the reader is drawn into a frightening hallucination. A book written in a state of delirium that lasted three months. There was nothing like it in Kubin's life before that moment; nothing like it after. The novel coincides perfectly with *something that happened* to the author on a particular occasion. There are two novels alone before Kafka that already breathe the air of Kafka: Kubin's *The Other Side* and Robert

Walser's *Jakob von Gunten*. Both were to find their place in the Biblioteca series. There was another reason for this: alongside the idea of the singular book, if we had to talk about a *singular author* for the twentieth century, one name would stand out: Kafka.

In short, a singular book is one in which it is clear that *something has happened* to the author and has been put into writing. At this point it should be noted that Bazlen had a marked impatience about writing. Paradoxically, considering that he spent his entire life among books, he regarded the book as a secondary result, which suggested there was something else behind it. The writer needed to live through this other thing, he needed to absorb it physiologically, preferably (though this did not have to happen every time) transforming it in style. If this had happened, these were the books that most attracted Bazlen. To understand this, it's worth remembering that Bazlen had grown up at a time when it was widely claimed that the pure literary word had a right to self-sufficiency, the years of Rainer Maria Rilke, of Hugo von Hofmannsthal, of Stefan George. And as a result he had developed certain allergies. The first time I saw him, as he was talking with Cristina Campo about her magnificent translations of William Carlos Williams, he insisted on only one point: "One shouldn't hear too much of the *Dichter* . . ." the "poet-creator," in the sense of Friedrich Gundolf and a whole German tradition that came down from Goethe (a tradition, by the way, of whose great significance Bazlen was, moreover, perfectly aware).

Singular books were therefore books that had also run a considerable risk of never having been written. From Zhuangzi (Bazlen's true master, if we had to name only one) it could be claimed that the perfect work is one that leaves no trace. Singular books were similar to the *residue, śeṣa, ucchiṣṭa*, about which the authors of the Brāhmaṇas never stopped speculating and to which the *Atharva Veda* dedicates a magnificent hymn. There is no sacrifice without residue—and the world itself is a residue. Books therefore have to exist. But it must also be remembered that, if the sacrifice had succeeded in leaving no residue, then there would never have been any books.

Singular books were books in which—in very different situations, periods, circumstances, ways—the Great Game was played out, in the sense of *Le Grand Jeu*, the name of the journal directed by René Daumal and Roger Gilbert-Lecomte. For Bazlen, those two turbulent adolescents, who at the age of twenty had set up a journal compared with which the Surrealism of Breton seems pompous, conceited, and often outdated, prefigured a new, strongly hypothetical anthropology toward which singular books were directed. An anthropology that still belongs, as much if not more than ever before, to a possible future. When 1968 erupted a few years later, I found it irritating at first, like an ungainly parody. Compared with *Le Grand Jeu*, this was a modest and compliant way of rebelling, as would become all too clear in subsequent years.

Mount Analogue, to which Daumal dedicated his

unfinished novel (which would become no. 19 in the Biblioteca series, accompanied by an illuminating essay by Claudio Rugafiori) was the axis—visible and invisible—along which the flotilla of singular books was tacking. But this should not suggest that each of these books was intended to express some kind of esotericism. *Father and Son* by Edmund Gosse, no. 2 in the Biblioteca series, would be enough to disprove the idea. A detailed, balanced, and harrowing account of a father-son relationship in Victorian times, it is the story of an unavoidable lack of understanding between two solitary beings, a young boy and an adult, who at the same time are capable of stern mutual respect. In the background: geology and theology. Edmund Gosse would later become a distinguished literary critic, but almost without any trace of that boy described in *Father and Son*, that being to whom *Father and Son* happens. *Father and Son*, as a memoir, therefore has something of the singularity of *The Other Side*.

Among such disparate books, what at this point could be the essential requisite that had nevertheless to be recognized? Perhaps just the "right sound," another expression that Bazlen sometimes used, as a final argument. No experience, in itself, was enough to bring a book into existence. There were many cases of fascinating and significant events that had nevertheless produced dull books. Here, too, an example comes to mind: many people were imprisoned, deported, and tortured during the last world war. But for a clear and simple account of the experience of total isolation and total defenselessness and how it can yield a discovery of something else, the book to read is *Solitary Confinement* by Christopher Burney (no. 18 in the Biblioteca series). And the author, after writing that book, would fade back into anonymity. Perhaps because he'd had no intention of writing a work, but that work (that singular book) had gone through him in order to come into existence.

Having chosen the name of the series, we now had to create its look. We immediately agreed on what we wanted to avoid: whiteness and graphic designers. Whiteness because it was the hallmark of Einaudi's design, which was the finest then in circulation—and not just in Italy. It was therefore essential to try to be as different as possible. And so we focused on color and on matte paper (our Imitlin, which we have used ever since). So far as colors were concerned, those used at that time in Italian publishing were relatively few and fairly awful. There was room to explore whole ranges of intermediate tones.

We also wanted to do without graphic designers. However good they may or may not have been, they all shared one defect: whatever they did looked immediately to be the creation of a graphic designer, following certain rather narrow-minded rules practiced by followers of the Modernist bible. We felt there were other ways. And one day a catalog of the work of Aubrey Beardsley began circulating around the office. At the back were several maquettes for book covers he had designed for the Keynotes series published by John Lane,

at Vigo Street, London, in 1895. With a few small adjust-
ments, and replacing the frieze that Beardsley added
along the black upper strip with "Biblioteca Adelphi,"
the cover was complete. Above all, it provided a template
for an element we regarded as essential: the image. And
so in homage to Beardsley we decided that no. 2 of the
series—*Father and Son*—should include the frieze that
Beardsley had created for *The Mountain Lovers* by Fiona
Macleod.

Many years later, in an antiquarian bookshop, I
was surprised to come across the publicity brochure for
the Keynotes series. And I could hardly believe my eyes
when I found reproduced there the cover designed by
Beardsley for *Prince Zaleski* by M. P. Shiel. What an ex-
traordinary coincidence . . . Totally forgotten in Britain,
M. P. Shiel was the author of *The Purple Cloud*, which
was perhaps Bazlen's last exciting discovery while he was
looking for books for Adelphi, and was also to become
one of the Biblioteca's first immediate successes. Published in 1967, masterfully translated and introduced
by J. Rodolfo Wilcock, it was reprinted straight away
and soon became one of those books—like *The Book of
the It* by Georg Groddeck—from which and in which the
first Adelphi readers became identified.

Name, paper, colors, graphic design: all essential
aspects of the series. Still missing was what makes a
book recognizable: the image. What did the image
on the front cover have to be? *The reverse of ekphrasis*—
that's how I would describe it today. And of course we
never described it in that way, but we proceeded as

though it were implicit. *Ekphrasis* was the term used in ancient Greece to indicate the rhetorical device that translated works of art into words. There are writings—such as Philostratus's *Images*—dedicated entirely to ekphrasis. In modern times, the supreme virtuoso of ekphrasis was Roberto Longhi. Indeed, it could be said that the boldest and most revealing aspects of his essays are his descriptions of paintings, far more than his discussion and analysis. But, Longhi aside, the unequaled master of ekphrasis is still Baudelaire, not just in prose, but also in verse. When he described Delacroix as a "lac de sang hanté des mauvais anges" ("lake of blood haunted by bad angels") or David as an "astre froid" ("cold star"), Baudelaire was showing just how precise and invaluable the word had managed to become in relation to those two painters. So the publisher who chooses a book cover—whether he realizes it or not—is the last, the most humble and obscure descendant in the line of those who practice the art of ekphrasis, but this time applied in reverse, attempting to find the equivalent or the *analogon* of a text in a single image. All publishers who use images practice the art of ekphrasis in reverse, whether they realize it or not. And even typographical book covers are an application of it, if only in a more limited and underhand form. And this is true irrespective of quality: as an art, it is no less important for a pulp fiction book than for a novel of great literary ambition. But here we need to add one crucial detail: it is an art on which there is a heavy onus. The image that is to be the *analogon* of the book must be chosen not for itself, but above all in relation to a vague and ominous entity who will judge it: the public. It is not enough for the image to be right. It has to be perceived to be right by a multitude of extraneous eyes, who generally know nothing about what they will find inside the book. A paradoxical situation, almost comical in its ramifications: an image has to be offered that will intrigue and encourage unknown people to pick up an object about which they know nothing except the name of the author (a name they are often seeing for the first time), the title, the name of the publisher, and the words on the cover flap (a text that is always suspect, since it is written *pro domo*). But at the same time the cover image must look right even *after* these unknown people have read the book, if only to stop them from thinking that the publisher doesn't know what he's publishing. I doubt whether many publishers have thought very much along these lines. But I know that all of them without distinction—the best and the worst—each day ask themselves one question that is more straightforward in appearance only: is this particular image selling or not? When considered closely, the question is more akin to a koan than to anything else. *To sell* indicates here an equally obscure process: how can you stimulate a desire for something that is a composite object, largely unknown and to an equally large extent elusive? In the United States and in Britain, teams of sophisticated art directors find themselves in this situation every day: they are given *an entity* (a book, which they haven't necessarily read), together with several primary and secondary characteristics (expected print run, type of target readership, subject matter and the issues it might raise). Their task is to create the image and the most effective packaging in which to present it. American and British books today are the result. Sometimes ugly, sometimes brilliant, but always following this pattern, so that they become too closely related to each other. It's as though all the book covers on display in a bookstall came from one same center, in which some departments are highly expert and others fairly inept. This system may or may not appeal. But so far as Adelphi is concerned, a very different system was always applied.

We felt, from the outset, that with a little perseverance we could find something each time from the sea of existing images—whether pictures or photographs or designs—that would be appropriate for the book we were about to publish. So we have never commissioned a front cover. For more than thirty years, Luciano Foà and I have sifted, tried, and retried hundreds and hundreds of images, formats, and background colors. Unfortunately, Bazlen was unable to take part in this game—he died in July 1965, the very same month that the printing of the first volume of the Biblioteca series was completed. But everyone involved in the publishing house took part, and still takes part in various ways. Including the author, when available. And every suggestion from outside is always welcome. For sometimes the choice is quite a headache. And there are plenty of regrets—and regrets about regrets. Just one example: when it came to the second edition of Gosse's *Father and*

Son we decided to change the front cover by replacing Beardsley's flowers with a splendid photo of Gosse father and son that, in the first edition, had been opposite the title page. Today I would perhaps prefer to return to the original.

The art of ekphrasis in reverse needs time—a lot of time—to develop, expand, breathe. The aim is to get a web of images that not only respond to a single object (the book for which they are being used) but also resonate with one another, similarly to the way that various books in the series can relate to one another. In this way, strange instances of irresistible affinity were created, so that certain authors attracted certain painters. For example, Georges Simenon and Léon Spilliaert. Spilliaert—a Belgian like Simenon, a still-underrated genius—began to appear on the jackets of Simenon books in 1991, with *The Man Who Watched the Trains Go By* (in our pocket series). And since then he has appeared there twelve times. Always leaving the impression, in us but also in our readers (as we have been able to confirm), that this was the *right* image. So each time we publish a Simenon in the Biblioteca series, we instinctively look for the most appropriate Spilliaert. If Simenon has always been celebrated as the creator of atmospheres, it can be supposed that something of those atmospheres filters onto Spilliaert's canvases or is already there waiting for Simenon the writer to describe them. What they share is something spare, lurid, sinister—a certain bleakness of background. And this might appear from a coat rack, a piece of old furniture, from the reflection in a mirror or from the sandy shore at Ostend.

But Spilliaert is also linked to another, very different author: Thomas Bernhard. Their story might help in understanding the strange resonances created by practicing ekphrasis in reverse. When the moment came for publishing the first of Bernhard's five-volume autobiography, I remember feeling unsure where to look. Bernhard is a prime example of those authors for whom it is very difficult to find an image to put on the front cover (and in fact Suhrkamp editions of his novels have always had typographic covers). It is as though his supreme idiosyncrasy extended to the realm of figures, repelling them. The choice finally fell on Spilliaert: the picture of a long, low wall, behind which is an expanse of yellowy-red sky and, to one side, the outline of a bare tree with dense branches. I couldn't explain why I thought that image was right for *The Origin*, a book centered around Salzburg, a baroque city infected by Nazism and bigotry. But it did not displease me. Two years later, we published the second volume of the autobiography, *The Cellar*. Once again I settled on a Spilliaert: several bare tree trunks in an empty landscape. Then came the third volume, *The Breath*—and it was another Spilliaert: a tall tree with many bare branches. A complicity, a secret alliance, had been created by this stage between Bernhard's autobiography and Spilliaert's trees. For the fourth volume, *The Cold*, another Spilliaert was to be seen on the front cover: an avenue in winter, lined by trees with bare branches. Having reached the last volume, *A Child*, once again I felt great uncertainty. I may not, in the end, have found any more trees by Spilliaert but the choice nevertheless fell on one of his pictures: it showed some colored boxes, stacked one on another. It was a strangely appropriate cover for that book, with something childish and also joyous, without having to refer to the figure of a child.

I met Bernhard a few times, each of them memorable. First in Rome, with Ingeborg Bachmann and Fleur Jaeggy in the early 1970s. Bernhard had given a reading from one of his works at the Austrian Institute. He told us how the director of the institute had been so eager to inform him, with Viennese formality, "The bed in which you will be sleeping is the one in which Johannes Urzidil died a few months ago." Bernhard remained silent that evening until well after midnight. Then, prompted to say something, he talked nonstop for several hours, telling a series of hilarious and generally macabre stories until dawn. The subject matter? The Irish, cemeteries, sleeping pills, farmers. By the time we had taken him back to the institute it was daybreak. Several years later, in Vienna, I delivered to him a volume of his autobiography that had just been published. He leafed through it, looked carefully at the print, and seemed pleased. Then he said the paper was good. Not a word more. And we began talking about something else. I should add that we never discussed books, least of all his books. That was the last time I saw him.

Shortly after his death, in July 1989, the publisher Residenz sent me a copy of Bernhard's *In der Höhe*. The author probably didn't live to see a finished copy of it. The book struck me as déjà vu. On the front cover: bare branches on a pale background, with a few delicate patches of color. It wasn't a work by Spilliaert but it could have been. The front cover was not on glossy paper—like that of every other Residenz book—but matte, of the kind we used. The page layout was exactly the same as that of Adelphi's Narrativa Contemporanea series in which the first volumes of the Bernhard autobiography had appeared. I telephoned Residenz and asked for an explanation of this change, which made it quite unlike all the publisher's other books. They told me it had been Bernhard's express wish. Indeed, he had made it a condition that the book should be presented in this way. I took it as a farewell gesture.

Over the years and through experience—by making mistakes and correcting them—various criteria began to develop in the search for appropriate images for the Biblioteca series: first of all, as a matter of principle, to avoid old masters, painters too identifiable and images too widely used, since some element of surprise—in the image itself or in its context—was an essential requirement (but in this, as in all the rest, there would be exceptions: hence Dürer's violets for Marina Tsvetaeva); and then to pick out certain painters who, regardless of when they lived, seem to have sensed, for reasons not easily discernible, some sort of vocation to become book covers, of which they perhaps wouldn't have approved (among these, William Blake); also to make good use of certain great artists who were underrated (such as Spilliaert) or never fully recognized (such as Félix Vallotton) or not yet widely appreciated (such as Vilhelm Hammershøi). Finally: to create a sort of club of kindred spirits, ready to give assistance in the most varied cases: George Tooker (for Milan Kundera, William Burroughs, Reiner Kunze, Vladimir Nabokov, Oliver Sacks, Leonardo Sciascia), Alex Colville (for Álvaro Mutis, Georges Simenon, Christina Stead, Robert M. Pirsig), Richard Oelze (for Gottfried Benn, Sacks, Burroughs, Varlam Šalamov, C. S. Lewis), Meredith Frampton (for Nabokov, Muriel Spark, Ivy Compton-Burnett, Henry Green).

Once these strategies are understood, once the several hundred images that have appeared on the front covers of the Biblioteca series over the course of fifty years are placed side by side, as if on an enormous table (especially if we add the covers of the two parallel Fabula and Gli Adelphi series), it shouldn't be difficult to see a sequence of lines that overlap with those of canonical art history, or produce a counterpoint or contrast to it. But these things ought not to be emphasized, except in passing. It is for readers to discover them, mentally retracing the paths and reasons that have led to certain combinations.

•

Vienna was very different before being discovered as
the Grand Vienna. In the sultry summer of 1968 the
shop windows were still piled high with ugly objects,
together with their prices, like a provincial city still
recovering from war. Works by Klimt and Schiele still
hung in the back rooms of antique shops. The only
people to talk about Karl Kraus were certain gentlemen
of exquisite manners who remembered being there
when his demon shook the city. One of them told me
how he had sold his complete collection of *Die Fackel* to
an American officer for a substantial quantity of ciga-
rettes. But Kraus's books were nowhere to be seen. They
were slowly being reprinted by a publisher called Kösel
who specialized in theology—noble editions, invisible
among the new publications. Working on Kraus, whom
I had the idea of translating, it became increasingly
clear that *his* Vienna was indeed that "cosmic point" of
the Sirkecke that he had once described—an astound-
ing galaxy that had emerged with the young Hofmannsthal in the guise of Loris, perfectly mature at the age
of eighteen, and which in all probability had been swal-
lowed up when Freud and his family, thanks to the
help of Marie Bonaparte, had succeeded in getting out
on a train for London, which might have been the last.
Between those two moments, a great many questions
and forms had passed along those streets that had remained unaffected by time. Indeed they were more apparent than ever before by reason of a certain firm
radicalism that hadn't been reached elsewhere. Schönberg and Wittgenstein, Musil and Gödel, Kraus and

Hofmannsthal, Freud and Roth, Schnitzler and Loos: they had all run into one another on the Graben, had brushed past or ignored one another, had often detested one another. But what bound them together was much stronger—and only now did it begin to emerge. Expressed in the most elementary formulation: in no other place than Vienna had the ultimate questions of language been so lucidly posed (which for Kraus could be the language of everyday life and newspapers; or for Gödel the language of formal systems; or for Schönberg the language of the tonal system; or for Freud the mysterious rebus of dreams).

The good fortune of the Biblioteca series began to become apparent when a certain number of readers discovered, book after book, that this constellation was taking form, with no exclusions of genre, within the same series. This phenomenon can be followed from reactions to Joseph Roth. In 1974 we published *The Emperor's Tomb* in an edition of 3,000 copies. Roth was a name that at that time meant nothing. The book was immediately reprinted, though still in the order of a few thousand copies. But soon it went beyond that threshold. *Flight Without End*, two years after *The Emperor's Tomb*, was immediately received with enthusiasm by a vast readership. And to our amazement we realized that, at a time when *literature* had become a dirty word, the novel was being covertly adopted by youth of the far Left. I remember some members of the Lotta Continua extremist party saying that it was the only story with which they could identify—or at least, with which they would have liked to identify, in that moment of turmoil. It would have been good if they had pursued Roth even further. And so, after another two years, in 1978, for a book that wasn't one of Roth's greatest, *The Silent Prophet*, we had to start off with a print run of 30,000 copies because so many bookshops were asking for it. And it was immediately sold out. On the front cover there was a Schiele, which still seemed usable without any second thoughts (it is hard to imagine there was a time when Schiele or Hopper were still *not* well known and on posters everywhere). The success, the real fashion for Joseph Roth in Italy, was due not only to the recognition of his great fascination as a storyteller, but to the fact that around him—and in the Biblioteca series itself—other stars in the Viennese constellation continued appearing. And the time would also come for more discreet and elusive literary authors, such as Peter Altenberg and Alfred Polgar. Or someone like Alexander Lernet-Holenia, an outstanding inventor of plots against whom his own culture of origin still stubbornly resists.

But it is also worth remembering another point that readers could hardly ignore, of an intensely editorial nature. If Joseph Roth's prose and phrasing have slipped so easily into the veins of the Italian language, it is thanks not so much to any one of his many translators, but to his *single editor*: Luciano Foà. Book by book, from *The Emperor's Tomb* (1974) to *The Ballad of the Hundred Days* (1994), Foà kept aside a certain number of weeks each year for *editing Roth*. For him it was a task that seemed obvious and natural. And the result was that precision of detail and that delicate patina that protected the whole of his writing, without which the peculiarity of Roth could not be understood. There were few writers whom Foà admired unreservedly. First among them were Stendhal and Kafka. And in Roth he recognized the writer who had come closest to Stendhal in the twentieth century.

The enduring link between Adelphi and *Mitteleuropa* was established between 1970 and 1980, in particular through a number of titles in the Biblioteca series. It began with Hofmannsthal's *Andrea*, followed by Karl Kraus, Adolf Loos, Ödön von Horváth, Joseph Roth, Arthur Schnitzler, Elias Canetti, and Ludwig Wittgenstein. And I notice that in 1980 Altenberg, Polgar, and Lernet-Holenia had not yet been published.

But memory plays strange tricks, superimposing images of things that happened at a later time and ignoring details that were then so vivid. It is therefore with some relief that I discovered several sheets of paper on which I jotted down some words of thanks I had given in September 1981 when the Austrian authorities were kind enough to award me the Ehrenkreuz *litteris et artibus* (and the word *Ehrenkreuz*, "cross of honor," immediately brought back to mind one of the most delightful pieces of prose by Kraus, in defense of a prostitute who had dared to pin on her breast that decoration, which had been given to one of her clients). I record these words of thanks here in full because they give some idea of how those events were seen at the time:

"Like all Italian children for about the past hundred years, I came across Austria for the first time as a child, in my primary school textbook that talked about Marshal Radetzky and described him as 'the beast.' So the beast Radetzky was the first Austrian I met. Then we learned Giuseppe Giusti's poem 'Sant'Ambrogio' by heart—and there we came across other unnamed Austrians, soldiers with tallow mustaches, poor folk 'in a country, here, that wishes them harm.'

"Fortunately for me, I have always tended to regard the things I read in history books as unreal. I therefore erased every overly exact image of Austria until one day, in 1957, when I was sixteen, I saw in the Hoepli bookshop in Rome the first volume of Robert Musil's *The Man Without Qualities*, published by Einaudi. The author was unknown to me, the front cover was a fine picture by Vuillard. Something attracted me immediately to the book: I was won over by the portrait of Leona, Ulrich's frivolous, gluttonous lover, who at the restaurant always orders *pommes à la Melville*. And, soon after, I was won over by the chapter that begins to describe Kakania as 'that misunderstood state that has since vanished, which was in so many things a model, though all unacknowledged.' In this country, whose name seems to come from an operetta but whose center of gravity was a great criminal called Moosbrugger, I at last encountered Austria, not just as a historical entity but as a place of

the mind. And that country gradually became populated for me, in its blend of nations and differences:
it was the land of Kafka and Schönberg just as much
as that of Loos and Kubin, of Altenberg and Schiele, of
Wittgenstein and Freud, of Polgar and Schnitzler.

"For me, that place was also populated by living
people, two of whom were crucial in my life: Roberto
Bazlen and Ingeborg Bachmann. Through them and
through those many invisible friends who are dead
writers, I was naturally led to experience those places,
those events, that fragile crystallization of civilization.
So when Adelphi began publishing its books, for which
it will be eternally indebted to Bazlen, we turned to these
authors I have mentioned with never a thought of just—
as they say—'filling a gap' or 'discovering a new line.'
Adelphi, as its name suggests, is a business based on
affinities: affinities between people as well as between
books. And it was for reasons of affinity that we often
turned to works in that Austrian sphere that I have
described.

"Reactions at first were slow and hesitant: not just
when we published Kubin in 1965 but even when we
published Kraus in 1972. One illustrious figure of the
publishing world [this was Erich Linder, at that time
the world's most important and certainly its most cul-
tured literary agent] predicted at the time that Kraus
would sell twenty copies. The book has now reached
its fourth edition. But the most obvious case of an infatuation for a great Austrian author was that of Joseph Roth, in relation to whom it can be said that Italy

is the only country where the surname Roth immediately evokes the name of the Austrian Joseph before
that of the American Philip. But I don't wish here to
go back over the fortune that many Kakanian authors
have had during these years, and in particular certain
books that Adelphi has published. I remember that
Alberto Arbasino once published an article in which he
said that Adelphi ought to be renamed Radetzky. That
day I had the impression of having turned full circle:
the beast Radetzky had become one of our totemic ancestors. His army, with their splendid uniforms, is an
army now dispersed, literary and invisible, whose last
surviving officer, without knowing it, is perhaps Fred
Astaire, whose real name was Frederick Austerlitz, the
son of an Austrian officer. This cross that I am receiving
today is for me, in a certain way, a sign that comes from
that invisible army."

Then there were certain books that seemed to have
been written especially for the Biblioteca series. One
day Angelica Savinio sent us an unpublished manuscript written by her father Alberto, who was the brother
of Giorgio de Chirico. It was the *Nuova enciclopedia*.
Dissatisfied by all encyclopedias, Alberto Savinio had
compiled one himself. The first entry: "abat-jour" ("lamp-
shade"). This would have been enough to win me over.
The book meandered on with countless intelligent and
witty remarks, in amiable tone, at times aloof and sar-
donic. Savinio had sought to transform the encyclopedic

form—essentially anonymous and collective—into the highest expression of idiosyncrasy: it is difficult to imagine a *singular book* that more exactly fits the definition. At that time, the only Savinio we had published had been *Maupassant e "l'Altro,"* an indefinable book, brimming with genius, which Debenedetti had already tried to publish in the Silerchie series. Otherwise, Savinio's work was not widely known, his name surrounded by a vast halo of silence. It never appeared in the literary annals. And yet he had known everyone, he had written tirelessly for leading newspapers and magazines. But an ancient, deadly spell was working against him. A nameless voice would keep on saying: "Savinio? Too intelligent." He seemed to lack that healthy obtuseness that some still regarded as the characteristic of a true artist. There were obviously other reasons for rejecting him. First of all, his ability to remain detached from the literary society around him, his unpredictable way of dealing with anything, from the *abat-jour* to the *zampirone* ("fumigator")—the penultimate heading in the *Nuova enciclopedia*. But these defects were exactly what made him so dear to us. And so Savinio entered full-sail into the Biblioteca series with his *Nuova enciclopedia*, which could be read as the encyclopedia most suitable for that composite tribe that had preceded him in the series.

With Joseph Roth we made a clear, decisive correction to our course. Bazlen's idea of the *singular book*, in its most radical form, went contrary to the idea of complete works. Bazlen was more interested in the moment, the individual expression, rather than the work in all its ramifications. It was a very bold, far-reaching idea—and one for which the times were not yet ripe. But what should we have done with Roth? *The Emperor's Tomb* was one of his greatest novels but, to really understand it, it had to be put in sequence with all the others, some of them no less fine. Roth, like few others, is the author of linked narratives. And so it happened, from 1974 to 1994, year by year, that we published *all* the narrative works of Roth (then continuing on with his magnificent journalistic articles). And in fact it was an approach that we would also apply, from then on, to other writers as soon as the rights situation allowed: to Blixen, Borges, Nabokov, but also to Maugham—and finally, with an impressive range of titles, to Simenon.

I was writing my observations about front covers when *The New York Times Magazine* published a long article by Kevin Kelly, described indeed as "a manifesto." Its title ("Scan This Book!") was immediately followed by the question "What will happen to books?" His byline referred to Kelly as "the 'senior maverick' at Wired magazine" and therefore authoritative by definition.

At first I thought it was yet another of those doomsday stories, almost comical to read today, that began appearing as soon as one of various, by now obsolete, electronic devices appeared. But in this case there was something more subtle, which could already be seen in the caption of a photo over the main title: "You can't judge a book from the cover if there's no longer a cover." Rather than the book itself, the focus was that strange object about which I was writing: the cover. The beginning of the article was indistinguishable from a thriller: "In several dozen nondescript office buildings around the world, thousands of hourly workers bend over table-top scanners and haul dusty books into high-tech scanning booths. They are assembling the universal library page by page." These lines already have a whiff of deportation and butchery. And we realize straight away that something very serious is going on, though we don't know whether it is to be admired or feared. The position becomes clearer with the next sentence: "The dream is an old one: to have in one place all knowledge, past and present." And since when did the old dream become a reality? Since December 2004, when Google announced that it would scan the books of five major research libraries (with Stanford, of course, at the forefront). The article continues, as it had to, with a few figures. "From the days of Sumerian tablets till now," we are told, "humans have 'published' at least 32 million books." This would be the basis of the "universal library." But immediately the devil butts in: "And why stop there? The universal library should include a copy of every painting, photograph, film and piece of music produced by all artists, present and past. Still more, it should include all radio and television broadcasts. Commercials too. And how can we forget the Web? The grand library naturally needs a copy of the billions of dead

Web pages no longer online and the tens of millions of blog posts now gone—the ephemeral literature of our time." These last, fanciful words are insufficient to wipe out the sense of terror and paralysis that the earlier words have already instilled. What has been described is perhaps the most advanced form of persecution: life besieged by a life in which *nothing is lost* and everything is condemned to exist, available always, suffocating. In this context, books seem like a far-off province or the realm of operetta. What are 32 million books in the face of phalanxes of billions of "dead Web pages" exponentially growing? These are the true living dead that besiege us. As I was reading, I thought: is there anyone who has gone farther than that? Yes there is: Joe Gould, the dazzling New York eccentric whose life was brilliantly captured by Joseph Mitchell. Gould was the man who claimed to have written the "oral history" of his time, that unknown history which includes every single word said in conversation in a bar (in all bars) or in a subway car (in all subway cars) or in any other place. In comparison with Joe Gould's plan, even that of Google is provincial and modest. And Kevin Kelly, in his enthusiasm, reveals the awkwardness of the novice. But precisely for this, for the lethal candor of his words, it is worth following Kelly's arguments. For example, what does technology want? Answer: "Technology accelerates the migration of all we know into the universal form of digital bits." The powerful ethnic migrations that are racking the globe are just the shadow of a vaster and all-pervading migration, which aims toward a "universal form." There is nothing exaggerated or inaccurate in all this. In fact, the world had been digitizing itself for centuries (or rather for millennia), but without knowing it, without saying it, without possessing a word that named what was happening. Digitizing is fundamentally nothing more than saying that *a* may stand for *b*. Then the word was formed. Its baptism in thought could be celebrated with *The Computer and the Brain* (1958) by John von Neumann. Then, in a matter of a few years, the world officially started to become digitized. And finally we came to the Google program, presented as an agent for *universal digitization*. If such is the focus, every other transformation will be subordinate to it, almost as though it were a secondary application.

But could everything proceed unhindered? Nothing proceeds unhindered. A contrite Kelly explains: yes, it's true, the digitization of books is proceeding rather slowly, "because of copyright questions and the physical fact of the need to turn pages." An invaluable observation, from which we find out who are the enemies: first, copyright as a legal limitation, and then the physical nature of the book itself, which demands certain specific gestures—such as, for example, *turning the pages*. But there is also something about the form of the book that is deeply detestable and old-fashioned: the cover. The cover is the skin of that body which is the book. And this is a serious obstacle for anyone wanting to start off the *partouze* of the universal library: a *partouze* that is never-ending and unstoppable, between bodies without skin. This is perhaps the most effective image if we want to cancel out any kind of erotic desire. Indeed, if we want to make eros repellent. But fortunately, continues Kelly, the Swiss have invented a robot that "automatically turns the pages of each book as it scans it, at the rate of 1,000 pages per hour." It is therefore to be hoped that the *partouze* will proceed at a faster pace from now on.

Like all American dreams, universal digitization is based on well-meaning sentiment and on a certain benevolence toward poor, distant foreigners—who, at the moment, serve above all to reduce the cost of digitization itself (Kelly, meticulous as ever, tells us that to scan a book today costs ten dollars in China and thirty at Stanford), but will one day have *access* (this is the magic word) to everything. And here Kelly risks sounding lyrical. Who will be the beneficiaries? "Students in Mali, scientists in Kazakhstan, elderly people in Peru." From this example it would seem that universal digitization can't do much to influence preset ideas about ethnic characteristics: Kelly would hardly have spoken about Peruvian scientists and elderly people in Mali. But this isn't the point. And it would be ridiculous to raise any objection over the lure that the sudden availability of an immense quantity of words and images might have upon someone who has difficulty even just *seeing* a book, an object that is exotic in so many parts of the world.

The point is that universal digitization implies a certain hostility toward a *way of knowledge*—and only as a consequence toward the object that embodies it: the book. It is not therefore a matter of being concerned about the survival of the book itself. The book has already encountered difficult times and has always endured. No one, after all, wishes it much harm. At worst, there's an attempt to treat it like an endangered species, to be corralled in a large natural park.

Instead, a fairly rigorous attempt is being made to get rid of a whole way of knowledge that is closely connected to the *use* of the book. More precisely, to get rid of a certain way of relating to the unknown. Here everything becomes harder and more risky. But why should the book have these powers? Why does the new digital sensibility find it so irritating, almost offensive as an object? Once again, all we have to do is follow Kelly to find the answer. First of all, books have the nasty defect of being "isolated items, independent from one another, exactly as they are on shelves in your public library" (more accurately in *any* library, public or private, from time immemorial). From this, Kelly insists that "each book is *pretty much unaware* of the ones next to it." This unawareness is already an antidemocratic attitude, a way to avoid sharing with others or *envers l'Autre* (if we were in France).

Books hadn't realized they were laden with so many prejudices since they were invented by Gutenberg. Then there is an aggravating factor: the author. "When an author completes a work, it is fixed and finished." As if to say: dead. In fact, "the only movement occurs when a reader picks it up to animate it with his or her imagination." Writers are, in essence, producers of corpses, which in certain cases can be subjected to galvanic experiments thanks to the intervention of external agents: the readers—who are, we soon discover, the true heroes of this whole new digital story. And not just certain readers but readers *in general*, this immense, invisible hive of activity that tirelessly intervenes, corrects, connects, labels. *Links* and *tags* are the crucial words here. According to Kelly, who doesn't like letting irony or doubt creep in, they "may be two of the most important inventions of the last 50 years." And, in their impending mass, readers are also those who will prevent books from indulging in their more pernicious tendency, that of *being an island*. Here Kelly's tone solemnly echoes John Donne: "In the universal library, no book will be an island."

The enemy is therefore the isolated, solitary, and self-sufficient existence of books. They are by nature asocial beings that have to be digitally reeducated. But scanning—warns Kelly—is just a first step, similar to the procedures when someone is taken to prison, shaved, and provided with a uniform: "The real magic will come in the second act, as each word in each book is cross-linked, clustered, cited, extracted, indexed, analyzed, annotated, remixed, reassembled and woven deeper into the culture than ever before." Which makes it sound like a bondage manual. The reader—or the anonymous programmer—is the insatiable dominatrix who wants the book to pay penance for all the sins it didn't know it had committed. But books have long been accustomed to suffering some of these torments, sometimes with a perverse pleasure—for example, those inflicted by indexes or concordances. After all, masochism is a fundamental, inalienable sentiment. Far more worrying, however, is the final operation to which Kelly refers: that of ensuring "every word in every book" is "woven deeper into the culture than ever before." Into what *culture*? It is well known that this word is now meaningless due to the excess of meanings given to it. And why should a book be "woven deeper" into it, however it might be construed? And what if that book had wanted to *unweave* itself from everything? Kelly's phrase evokes a feeling of asphyxia. We no longer feel protected by the neutral, asemantic whiteness of the paper on which the letters of a book are printed. Letters have now invaded all empty space, stuck like flies on flypaper.

Or, what is more, the whole process tries to circumvent a certain way of relating to the unknown. For someone reading a page of a book, beyond the letters is the whiteness of the page, which is mute and recalls the stubborn muteness of the world that surrounds the book. But in front of a screen everything changes: here a page can also be substituted, modified, extended by another page, and so on, more or less ad infinitum. And one is tempted to ignore the mute background, as if the whole world were made only of letters (or images) substituting other signs. As a result, the role of the unknown is enormously reduced—and this is enough to change the character of knowledge itself. Having reached this point, even the maverick Kelly feels he must pause before the majesty of what he is revealing. The text—any text—is a pretext. What matters is the *link*, the connection. And there is nothing like numbers to give an idea of this: "There are about 100 billion Web pages, and each page holds, on average, 10 links. That's a trillion electrified connections coursing through the Web." At this point I felt a pang: how would those "connections" that Kelly had just mentioned be translated into Sanskrit? They would be the *bandhus* of which the Vedic seers spoke. The world and the thought about the world—the one and the other—were made, they said, with those *bandhus*. And the most mysterious *bandhu* was the one that linked the unmanifest to the manifest, the *asat* to the *sat*. I felt a sense of amazement, as if I were trapped in a hallucination. Implicit in all I have written was the conviction that we are experiencing—day after day, and more and more as we move ahead—*the inversion of origin*. The Vedic view of *bandhus* is the closest we can get to an origin that has left its trace in words (in this case the *Ṛgveda*). And now we see it reappear in a sweeping parody in the words of someone who seems unaware of the existence of the Vedic seers—and who at the same time reports accurately on something undeniable, which is all around us. But, of course, the parody involves an inversion of meaning.

With the vision of the trillion *connections* coursing through the Web, Kelly must have felt he was getting close to "the bottom of things." Which he describes thus, in a tone of sinister camaraderie: "Once text is digital, books seep out of their bindings and weave themselves together. The collective intelligence of a library allows us to see things we can't see in a single, isolated book." But how does all this happen in practice? Once again, Kelly comes to our aid: "When books are digitized, reading becomes a community activity. Bookmarks can be shared with fellow readers. Marginalia can be broadcast. Bibliographies swapped. You might get an alert that your friend Carl has annotated a favorite book of yours. A moment later, his links are yours. In a curious way, the universal library becomes one very, very, very large single text: the world's only book." The more affable his tone, the more terrifying the prospect. What has happened? When he says that "reading becomes a community activity," it is implied that the secret, impenetrable, separate, discriminating, silent thought of the individual brain that reads has been replaced by *society*: an immense, all-pervading brain consisting of all brains, whatever they are, provided they operate and speak through the Web. It is a concentrated babble that creates a new kind of unrelenting background noise, unfortunately crowded with meanings.

The fundamental inversion that takes place is exactly this: that-which-is (whatever it may be) is replaced by the society of those who live and speak, pressing buttons and digitizing whatever they say inside that-which-is. The *Liber Mundi* is replaced by "the world's only book," accessible only online. As for the world, it is canceled out, superfluous, in its mute, refractory extraneousness. And the most worrying point of all, a final mark of the parody, is that while he was writing these words, Kelly was assuming the benevolent tone of someone picturing a group of old university friends who exchange notes and photographs and who enjoy helping each other out.

The legal dispute around the Google plan, started in fall 2005 by the Authors Guild and five American publishing groups, has now reached a first judgment and will presumably not last less than a generation. The legal problems that it raises are of the greatest interest, but all have to be considered as one consequence, among many, of a sort of radical oscillation of the mind, which is due to the process of universal digitization. In comparison to previous shocks in the framework of the mind, this has an entirely new peculiarity. First of all, *analog* and *digital* are not historical or cultural categories like so many before them. Analog and digital are primarily physiological categories, relating to the functioning of the brain at every instant. As I write these words and read them at the same time, analog and digital operations are occurring simultaneously in my mind, as in the minds of everyone else. These two poles are in perpetual conflict and are perpetually seeking an equilibrium, a balance, or a way of submitting or avoiding each other. The fact that this conflict has been trans-ferred, for the first time, into an immense prosthesis—the Web, which resembles the maze of connections in the brain—creates an unprecedented disruption that no one is particularly interested in recognizing. Like the millipede, we don't want to know too much about how these minuscule legs of our mind are moving at this moment. Because we know we'll end up paralyzed. But a moment will also come when it will be inevitable to think what we don't want to think. And then per-haps the temporary paralysis may prove beneficial.

It's time now to return to front covers. In Kelly's article there's a phrase that relates directly to them. A phrase that stands out, to the extent that it has been used to caption a large photo: a view from above of an impressive series of shelves filled with books: "What is the technology telling us? That copies don't count any more. Copies of isolated books, bound between inert covers, soon won't mean much."

Words that sound like a death sentence for the book itself. But why pick on the covers, describing them as "inert"? Can a cover be "inert"? No more than any other piece of paper. And we know that certain pieces of paper can develop a lethal energy. Why then so much disdain for the covers? Because they isolate the book from everything else, like the skin of every living being. And they isolate it in a highly analogical way, because the skin and what appears on the skin is the most powerful *analogon* of the being that it contains. But it is precisely this that cannot be accepted in the world of universal digitization. The cover reminds us that the mind can also act in an analogical way, allowing digitality to grow there with it. The cover is an indication—one of many—of the obstinate, mute, desperate resistance to the process that seeks to make "all the books in the world become a single liquid fabric of interconnected words and ideas": something similar to a paradise from which to escape at once, before being strangled and submersed at the same time in that "liquid fabric."

But what is Kelly's dream—and that of the vast tribe that can be glimpsed behind him? I ask because in America the word *dream* inevitably crops up at some point. And it is felt that the "dream" has to be something good and fine.

I have had to recognize with a certain shudder that Kelly's dream ends up in the same two words that I have been writing about: the *singular book*. Universal digitization should in the end swathe Earth in an impenetrable film of signs (words, images, sounds). And this would no longer be the *Liber Mundi* of medieval mystics, of Leibniz and Borges, but something much more daring: the *Liber Libri*, the all-enveloping emanation that, starting from a single digitized page, goes as far as covering everything like a *single book*. At that point the world could even disappear for being superfluous. And in any event it would be replaced by *information* on the world. And such information could also be, for the most part, *wrong*. The most effective and appropriate universal conspiracy in such a situation would be one that compelled its followers to send out on the Web only information that was false. Francis Bacon, champion of progress, spoke of truth being the daughter of time, *veritas filia temporis*, but—as Hans Blumenberg added—he could equally well have said, as soon emerged from the writings of Pierre Bayle: *error filius temporis*. The simple abolition of front covers has taken us such a long way.

What did publishing look like when Adelphi first appeared on the scene? Animated, confused, somewhat irresponsible, gracious. A sense of curiosity prevailed. Italian publishing in the 1950s meant only one thing: Einaudi. High quality, highly selective. But now everyone was tired of being taught selectivity. They wanted to find things out for themselves. And the dominant feeling was that somewhere there was still much to be discovered. "A vast part of what is essential," I once said. And someone took offense. But that "vast part of what is essential" had been missing in Italy for a very long time. More or less from the time of the early romantics. *Il Conciliatore* had *not* been the equivalent of the *Athenaeum* published by Novalis and the Schlegels. Italy over the past one hundred and fifty years had had a history of great solitary figures—like Leopardi, like Manzoni—trapped in a petty, asphyxiating fabric. Suffice it to compare average nineteenth-century Italian language with the equivalent French, English, or German. The Italian is read with difficulty, with embarrassment, it is overblown and at the same time rigid. The French, English, or German is often hard to distinguish from the prose of a hundred years later. They were languages that aged much better.

Apart from Einaudi (which was rapidly moving ahead in new directions, while maintaining its own codes—though less overtly), there was now Il Saggiatore, run by Giacomo Debenedetti, and also Feltrinelli and Boringhieri. But surprises could come from any quarter, depending on the spirit of the editorial directors: from Garzanti, Longanesi, Rizzoli, Mondadori, or Bompiani. Seen through the eyes of today, it all seems rather idyllic—and it certainly was not. But it's true there were still entire continents to discover, after having been subject to the Fascist Ministry of Popular Culture for twenty years and Comrade Ždanov for fifteen in the Italian variant of Sovietism. We could read the culture page of *Il Giorno*, which was far better than any that came after. Here Pietro Citati and Alberto Arbasino lavished their intelligence and insolence unstintingly, and weren't frightened of showing enthusiasm at times. Sometimes even a story by Carlo Emilio Gadda could land, like a meteorite, on the pages of the newspaper, in tiny print.

"And politics?" someone is bound to ask. How did Adelphi *fit in*? Quite simply, it didn't. There was nothing more tedious and exhausting than the disputes over the cultural hegemony (or dictatorship or enlightened reign) of the Left during the 1950s in Italy. It is an argument over which there ought to be nothing more to say. But it is always useful to set things out, for those whose memory tends to fail them and those born later. And, if possible, to set things out as swiftly and succinctly as possible, so as to avoid becoming tedious.

On a bookstall I happened to find an issue of *Nuovi Argomenti* that brought back memories of adolescence. It was dated March–April 1957 and bore the title "8 Questions on the Leader State." The answers were given by Mario Alicata, Antonio Banfi, Lelio Basso, Giuseppe Chiarante, Ernesto De Martino, Franco Fortini, Roberto Guiducci, Lucio Lombardo-Radice, Valdo Magnani, Alberto Moravia, Enrica Pischel, and Ignazio Silone. They range from the head of cultural policy for the Italian Communist Party (Mario Alicata) to the world's best-known Italian writer of the time (Alberto Moravia), who was also co-editor of the journal. That issue must have been meant as a bold critical initiative by several intellectuals, six months after the Hungarian Uprising.

An innocent reader of today might imagine, under the circumstances, that it would have addressed what had happened in Budapest. But there's no trace of this in the eight questions. Instead, the first went like this: "In what way do you think the USSR reconciles its role as leader state of international communism with the need for its policy of power?" From the answers it

could be gathered that a writer of international fame
(Moravia), a philosopher (Banfi), an anthropologist (De
Martino, the solitary representative of this profession
in Italy at that time), and a poet (Fortini) were all concerned, before anything else, about the health of the
"leader state." They could therefore talk about sedition
by troublemakers where this might help to emphasize
certain problems and needs of the "leader state." What
is most striking in those pages—apart from the same
leaden phrasing shared by the various authors—is the
fervor with which all are eager to come to the assistance of the "leader state," perhaps making a few tacit
objections, but always in the end wishing it well in its
mission.

It would be easy to pull more or less every paragraph
of that pamphlet to pieces. But the eye is eventually led
to the page where Lucio Lombardo-Radice (I remember his chubby pink face, like an eternal schoolboy)
talks, in relation to the events in Hungary, about "mas-
sacres of Communist militants, widely documented (and
celebrated!) by the bourgeois press." As we can see,
Lombardo-Radice was not afraid of strong words. And
he also spoke of *crimes* and *wrongs*. But which—and
whose? His allegations were serious: "Too many crimes
and too many wrongs of conservative reformism have
been committed and are being committed in the name
of 'socialism.'" The crimes and the wrongs were therefore directed *against* the "leader state." And an example
of this is given soon after, where Pietro Nenni is condemned for having dared to suggest a "verbal separation

of responsibility from the Soviet Union" (a significant nicety is the adjective *verbal*). In short, with manly firmness Lombardo-Radice was exhorting us to close ranks against those slandering the USSR (all *reformists*, a word that anyone today would be happy to use as a way of describing himself but then sounded like a grave insult). These were still the days when George Orwell's name was pronounced with a sense of disgust. He was, after all, a renegade.

Was Lombardo-Radice perhaps a crude and boorish Soviet agent? On the contrary, he was a perfect representative of that terribly *respectable* Italian intellectual elite—I say it without irony—who went from the circle of Benedetto Croce to that of Piero Calamandrei and the Partito d'Azione. Quite a number of the offspring of that family moved to the Italian Communist Party. But this fact had never scandalized anyone. Lombardo-Radice was one of them. He was the son of an eminent pedagogist, married to the daughter of a great Catholic jurist, Arturo Carlo Jemolo, and I remember him as being kind and amiable. But I'm not at all sure how he would have behaved if the followers of the "leader state" had come to power during that period. And as we know, children can be ferocious enough.

All in all, Adelphi emerged unscathed from the political turmoil of the first fifteen years. Those who disliked us—not so few—simply couldn't figure us out. The same publishing company that was accused of being elite would be accused a few years later, by the same people, of being too commercial. And the same authors were used as an example in both cases. Joseph Roth was one of these. When anyone, moreover, is accused of being a "Gnostic," then the fog really has set in. The word *gnostic* has, for centuries, been used to define everything that eludes current thought. And so *foetor gnosticus* is an honorable title, like *foetor judaicus*.

But someone at last appeared whose ideas were clear. He was anonymous, by necessity, like all those who wrote in *Controinformazione*, the official journal of the Red Brigades. It was a journal sold freely in all kiosks, alongside *Espresso* and *Panorama*, with a more limited but faithful readership. These details are worth recalling. In the June 1979 issue, in addition to the usual bulletins and declarations from prison, *Controinformazione* offered a long article with an ambitious title: "The Avant-Garde of Dissolution." It also had headings above and below: "Cultural counterrevolution and psychological war" and "Community aggregation, values of scarcity, social consensus in the long march of the everyday spectacle." Words very much of their time. As always in the writings of the Red Brigades, the starting point was rather remote. But, perhaps to help the reader, the essay was laid out in various sections, preceded by an introductory heading that summed it all up: " 'Refluence,' return to the past, refuge in the sacred, religious reawakening, return to the country, alternative workshops, naturalist ideologies, false environmentalism, psychological cycle of 'illusion-disappointment-frustration,' irrationalism, orientalist fervor, neo-clownist attitudes, body language, discovery of private identity: they are not just fashions, expressions of partiality, least of all 'deviations' to be resolved with healthy repractice of militant orthodoxy. On the contrary these 'deviations' are the concrete result, 'transversal,' endemic of a wider project theorized, promoted, and carried out by the centers of reaction." Within the limits of a certain vocabulary, it couldn't be clearer. And the final sentence struck a sorrowful note: "While so many tend toward isolated self-indulgence, the spiral machine of death advances engulfing a notable potential for antagonism."

The reader immediately felt goaded and wanted to know what were the "centers of reaction" (an updated version of the famous "dark reactionary forces lying in wait"). But the writings of the Red Brigades are always hard going at the start. And so, to reach the revelation, one had to wait until the ninth section, entitled "The Adelphi 'Case.'"

This is how it begins: "On a cultural level, similar and definitely more refined is the enormous work of other aspects of the counterrevolution, namely of publishing houses, among which Adelphi stands out for its solidity and presence, linked financially to the multinational capital of FIAT." And, already in the last lines of the previous section, Adelphi had been described as a "golden supporting structure of the superstructural counterrevolution." There was therefore esteem and respect for the enemy—and this is immediately repeated:

"The Adelphi production is learned, its books on offer captivating, its penetration subtle. Disconcerting is its *total* resilience which spreads over a range of excellent authors—for literary and philosophical depth—to whose fascination revolutionaries themselves yield devotedly." This was followed by a sentence that left me amazed: "In the Adelphi production chain the individual author is a link, a detail, a segment." Apart from the grotesque expression—the "production chain" was being operated along a corridor a few meters in length in Via Brentano, in the center of Milan—the anonymous sectarian had grasped something that official critics had not yet noticed: the *connection*, not immediately visible but very strong, that existed among the Adelphi titles—and particularly among those of the Biblioteca series. And here one immediately reached the nub of the argument, which was expressed like this: the *line* of the publishing house was said to be "aimed at undermining the principles of social revolt, at the mortification of collective revolutionary hope, at the invalidation of possible concerted subversion." The subverters discovered themselves to be victims of subversion, like the gardener with a hose who himself gets sprayed in the Lumière brothers' film. The terrorists felt terrorized—and were complaining of being subjected to a treatment (note the ominous noun *invalidation*, much used in the language of terrorism at that time) that was similar to what they handed out to their victims. It was necessary here to point out an example of such *subversion of subversion*. And it was Pessoa: "It will be appropriate to illustrate the observations on Adelphi's projects and purposes by referring to the latest success of this editorial gang: the publication of the works of Fernando Pessoa, the great Portuguese writer, translated for the first time in Italy (*Una sola moltitudine*)." Just a few years later, Pessoa was to be found, with his spectacles and hat, on the Portuguese escudo, the only twentieth-century writer who had succeeded in becoming a banknote. And his name today is passing through that difficult and perverse process at the end of which—as has already happened to Kafka and Borges—he will become a notion used above all by those who have never read his books. But at that time his name was generally unknown. It now seems unlikely but that was how it was: the volume of Pessoa edited by Antonio Tabucchi was greeted by a compact silence when it was published. Only the anonymous *Controinformazione* had recognized its importance. And it had drawn its own conclusions: Pessoa was the last incarnation of the *principal enemy*, who distracted and corrupted the last disciples of subversion. And the tone precipitated into that of an epicedium: "Thus, in Pessoa, the struggle draws to an end, the vital subversive energy is buried." The evil design of the "superstructural counterrevolution" is accomplished through the master of heteronyms.

Six hundred books in a single series is an enormity if we think how many fewer there were in Montaigne's tower or Spinoza's study. Six hundred books are enough to form a vast and varied mental landscape. Perhaps one of those Flemish landscapes where the most significant events are to be seen far in the distance, in marginal areas, where we see minuscule figures wandering about. It is a landscape where it is easy to get lost.

I wonder how readers who have only just learned to read will feel, when their time comes, in that landscape. Perhaps they won't like it and will want to leave straight away—in which case I'd be very curious to follow them. But I think they couldn't fail to recognize a certain constancy and recurrence in its features, however disparate. We could do a test, taking the first titles of 2006—the forty-first year of the Biblioteca series.

Elizabeth Bishop had to be one of those about whom Cristina Campo had written in *Gli imperdonabili*. And she is to be found alongside Marianne Moore, who was closest to her in life. The Confucius of Simon Leys fits in with the *Tao Te Ching* and *The Book of Lord Shang* translated by J.J.L. Duyvendak—two completely different Sinologists, one Dutch and the other Belgian, who, with precision and sobriety, seek to interpret immense and complex ancient Chinese texts. Simenon's *Cargo* followed upon twenty-three other "non-Maigret" novels by the same author. With him the rule of the singular book was reversed: it is not the individual title that is singular, but the entire *corpus* of novels, in their multiplicity and range. *David Golder* by Irène Némirovsky is linked with the painful stories of another Russian in Paris at the same time: Nina Berberova. And the characters from the stories of one could easily be moved into those of the other. And so on, for each title.

In his conversations with Eckermann, Goethe had referred to the idea of *Weltliteratur*: "universal literature" as the ineluctable prospect for all that is written. "National literature now means little, we are entering the period of universal literature and each must contribute toward hastening the arrival of this period."

Thus came the period not just of literature, but of universal hybridization. And Borges, through his entire work, would have added: everything can be regarded as literature. This today is the phantom ship that transports all possible combinations of forms and gathers them together on a neutral, impartial basis that is not a screen but a hypothetical mind. And it is perhaps one of the rare privileges of our time that this fact, daring in itself, has penetrated into the general awareness, unhindered. Literature is now either no longer noticed (the normal situation) or is hardly distinguishable from everything else. It is also for this reason that those six hundred titles of the Biblioteca Adelphi could be brought together and their juxtaposition didn't seem to jar or clash. To move from any one title to all the others became a plausible option for every reader, as it had been for those who helped to bring them together within the same framework. And this, after all, is the hidden purpose behind the idea of a series, and for the Biblioteca series in particular: to be taken literally, so that each bead stays linked to all the others along the same thread.

•

It was crucial for the fortunes of the Biblioteca series that a certain complicit relationship was established with its mysterious, composite, and perceptive readership. Various examples could be given, but the most spectacular came with Simenon.

When I went to meet him at Lausanne in fall 1982, together with Daniel Keel and Vladimir Dimitrijević (the first Simenon's publisher in German; the other the greatest expert on Simenon I have ever met), the situation concerning his books in Italy was as follows: many Maigrets, published in paperbacks and found in station kiosks, but none of the "non-Maigrets," or "hard novels" as Simenon called them. Many had obviously been published, starting from the 1930s, considering that Mondadori had been Simenon's first major foreign publisher. But all had gradually gone out of print. Simenon hadn't realized this was how things were, and he was surprised. I explained that our plan was to publish the "non-Maigrets" in the Biblioteca series, presenting them as the work of one of the finest storytellers of the century.

This was just the beginning, since there were contractual obstacles. I had almost lost hope of finding a solution when Simenon—notoriously drastic in dealing with publishers—finally let me know, two years later, that we could go ahead. And the deciding factor was, I believe, a long letter from Federico Fellini in support of our plan. Between Fellini and Simenon there was a complete understanding. And Fellini knew Simenon's work like no one else in Italy.

Our first Simenon, published in April 1985, was *Letter to My Mother* in the Piccola Biblioteca series. We published it not only because it is a passionate, highly intense piece of writing, but for a reason that concerned the author. Simenon was in fact upset that Mondadori had steadfastly avoided publishing that small book, claiming it was "too short." The *Letter* did not have an immediate success, even if some—few—recognized it as a revelatory text.

But we knew very well that the success of the Simenon experiment could only be judged on the outcome of the "non-Maigret" novels. If we had been Einaudi in the 1950s, we would have immediately looked for someone to write a preface to justify the operation and to direct the reader toward a proper understanding of the author. But Adelphi had never been inclined toward contextualization and pedagogy, which inevitably went with a certain paternalism toward the reader. We therefore decided to present Simenon as one of the great writers of the twentieth century, taking this for granted. And it can't be said to have been a widely held view at that moment: Simenon today is found in the Bibliothèque de la Pléiade, but then—even in France—his name didn't often appear in the literary annals.

It wasn't easy to choose which novel to begin with. I discussed it at length with Dimitrijević—and in the end the choice fell on *The Window over the Way*. Above all because it was one of Simenon's most perfect novels, almost forgotten in France and unknown in Italy. But there was another reason. Published in 1933 and set in Batum on the Black Sea, it described Soviet Russia in a way that no one had previously managed to do. When he wrote it, Simenon—the master of atmosphere, as he would so often be called—had just had a fleeting encounter with the Soviet Union. His wife, Tigy, in her recollections of the year 1933, noted: "In June we sail toward Turkey: Istanbul, Ankara; then southern Russia: Black Sea coast, Odessa, Yalta, Sebastopol, Batum. The novel *The Window over the Way* will describe clearly to what point the Russian atmosphere is depressing, distressing, unsafe. Betrayal, mistrust are the rule. We risked being detained and kept at Batum. It seemed our visas were not in order. Fortunately the caviar is amazing. Interview with Trotsky at Prinkipo."

But that was enough for Simenon. With his formidable antennae, he had *felt the air* of Soviet Russia, with the pure art of storytelling he had immediately entered into the veins of that overwhelming police and persecutory system that, twenty-four years later, some of the most respectable Italian intellectuals would describe as the "leader state." It was a case of visionary precision, of which not many would have been capable.

The Window over the Way was published in October 1985 with a print run of 9,000 copies. We were all very curious to see what would be the press reaction. And the crucial signal came immediately. In mid-November, an article by Goffredo Parise appeared in the culture section of *Il Corriere della Sera* under the heading "Georges Simenon and the 'Metaphysical' Crime Story," which I read with a vague sense of disbelief, for everything I had hoped would be noticed, not just in the book but in the way it was presented, was said with great elegance and incisiveness. The point of departure was the inside flap and the front cover (in this case a picture by Carel Willink, which was *not* a Black Sea landscape). And by introducing strictly editorial considerations into his comments, Parise went straight to the heart of the book: "Written around the 1930s by a genius, this short masterpiece is a book about police, control, the total annihilation of man under the most powerful, important, and demiurgic police dictatorship that modern man has ever known." A little later, with a masterly touch, Parise referred to "scenes, customs, and names that appear covered by the powder white of surrealist and metaphysical painting." The same *powder white* that covers the buildings painted by Willink in the picture on the cover.

After that article by Parise, I don't remember anyone daring to question whether Simenon could properly be considered one of the finest storytellers of the twentieth century. And Parise's enthusiasm must have infected a considerable number of readers since the forty-five subsequent novels were launched on the average basis of an initial print run of 50,000 copies.

In his article, Parise dwelt at length on the curious

phenomenon where an ordinary reader in a bookshop, having found and browsed through a book he knows nothing about, reaches the point where, "so greatly attracted by the book, he picks it up and takes it home impatient to read it. He reads it and discovers it's a masterpiece. Why does everything fit? First of all because the publisher has discovered a genuine masterpiece by reading it himself and not handing it out to be read: and in this way the front cover and the flap follow naturally from the masterpiece, inspired and strengthened by it. And by the same process the reader picks up the book, rushes home, puts everything else to one side, immerses himself in reading it, and discovers for himself that it's a masterpiece. Simple, isn't it? And yet it seems to be extremely difficult for the publisher of today, so difficult that when it happens there's great exultance."

The process described by Parise implied that there was a relationship of complicity between publisher and reader. A relationship that the marketing experts, in their unfathomable wisdom, define as "added brand value," an expression they feel to be more appropriate. How can that relationship be established? Complicity with unknown people can be created only on the basis of their repeated experiences of not being disappointed. But how can we be sure not to disappoint? It is practically impossible when dealing with a multitude of unknown people as vastly disparate as those who can pick up a book. It's better not to try. Or at least to limit ourselves to one basic rule: to think that what has not disappointed us (meaning that minuscule group that forms the mind of a publishing house) will not disappoint others. If this rule is applied, the result (the published book) will be highly idiosyncratic, to such an extent that many won't even pick it up, purely through lack of interest. And these are exactly the readers who would certainly feel disappointed. The others remain: very few, generally speaking. But those few can also become many. These are like-minded people who are perhaps attracted, Parise would have said, by a cover picture, which provides "a way of re-creating, through the illustration, the atmosphere or *Stimmung* of the book." And these will be the ones who are not disappointed, with whom the publisher, over time, can establish a tacit alliance.

One might object, at this point, that Simenon's work has such intrinsic energy and such a broad penetrative power that certain results should come as no surprise. It is hard to understand, then, why the same effects are not produced—for the "non-Maigret" stories we are describing here—in the United States or in Britain or in Germany, or in France itself. The way in which books are presented and the context in which they appear—which may be denoted by a simple typographical frame—still evidently have some importance. The essential role of the publisher is exactly this. So long as this complicity is successfully established, publishing will remain a fascinating game. But if one day, which many hope will be soon, all this becomes superfluous, for single books as well as single readers, we would indeed be entering another era. We would then also need to find a different way of defining the very act of reading. And certainly other books would be read.

I remember the first time I met Father Giovanni Pozzi. It was 1976 and a new series of Italian classics, the Ricciardi-Einaudi, was being presented. Discussions proceeded for some time along fairly predictable lines, including the inevitable complaint about the indifference of Italian readers toward their own literature. And here Father Pozzi intervened with a vehemence and passion that seemed to me admirable. It wasn't a matter, he said, of deploring a general indifference of readers, but of finding out first of all what they are indifferent to. What readers find today on the shelves of bookshops is *not* Italian literature but one fairly limited *section* of it, to which such literature has been reduced by the combined efforts of Italianists and publishers. What remains outside this area is enormous. Pozzi then gave various examples. He cited first of all religious literature, which has been part and parcel of Italian literature as far back as its origins and today is largely ignored. It goes without saying that I entirely agreed with him. But I was also struck by another point: standing before me was a great philologist, a great critic, and also a true *homo religiosus*— and each of the three aspects fitted together in a way that naturally strengthened the others. I thought then, as I do now, that mysticism is after all an exact science, as the Vedic seers well knew—and every other kind of exactitude is derived from it.

Alongside Father Pozzi I would like to place another figure, that of Roberto Bazlen, who devised the first program for Adelphi in the early 1960s. First of all, I would say that Bazlen was perhaps the most religious man I have known and certainly the least sanctimonious. He was immensely well read, but in the end he was fascinated by only one kind of book, in whatever form it was and to whatever period or civilization it belonged: that kind of book that is an experiment in knowledge, and as such can be transmuted into the experience of those who read it, thereby transforming that experience. I realize that in this way I have also defined the *animus* as well as the *anima* of the religious books published by Adelphi: works chosen not just in compliance with some cultural obligation, not just because they represent a sort of spiritual UNESCO, which is the exact opposite of all we have always stood for, but because they carry a possibility of knowledge without which our lives would simply be poorer.

I realize I have put the emphasis on the word *knowledge* without ever referring to that other word *faith*, which we generally encounter first, even in the dictionaries, when talking about religion. But I certainly don't wish to ignore the difficulty posed by this theological virtue. The reason for the temporary omission is this: paradoxically the word *faith*, due to the semantic wear it has suffered, often ends up becoming a hindrance rather than a help in considering religious ideas in the way I intended. To the point where, in order to associate it with the word *knowledge*, I feel I have to translate it into Sanskrit. The Vedic seers spoke of *śraddhā*, which means "trust in the effectiveness of ritual gestures." And here an explanation is necessary: "ritual gesture," for the Vedic seers, meant first of all "mental gesture." A mental gesture that was basically perpetual, in the same way that the ritual gesture, in the Vedic vision, occupied the whole of the year, and therefore of time. All of this can be easily retranslated into terms that are closer to us: what in fact is the continuous prayer referred to by an anonymous Russian in *The Way of the Pilgrim* if not a perpetual mental gesture? And what does this "mental gesture" imply if not the virtue of abandonment to Divine Providence? But I would also like to give another example, which could be described as the "primal scene" of *śraddhā*, of this singular form of faith. The first book I had the opportunity of translating and publishing for Adelphi, in 1966, was the autobiography of Saint Ignatius of Loyola. A brief, rough text dictated by the saint in his final years to his follower Gonçalves da Câmara and passed down to us in an edition that is half Castilian and half Italian. It is a swift and austere account, which retains the breath of oral narration. We know that in his youth Saint Ignatius was a man-of-arms with a violent character and a passionate reader of the tales of chivalry. One day, while already in the throes of religious conversion, but still racked by various torments, Saint Ignatius was riding a mule on the road to Montserrat. And here I hand over to him: "And so, as he continued on his way, he met a Moor who was riding a mule; and as they talked, they began to speak of Our Lady; and the Moor said it seemed to him that the Virgin had conceived without man; but he could not believe she had given birth while remaining a virgin and, as proof of this, he gave the natural causes that came to mind. The Pilgrim could not shift him from that opinion, however many reasons he gave. And so the Moor continued on his way with so much haste that the Pilgrim lost sight of him, and continued thinking about what had happened with the Moor. He was then overwhelmed by urges that brought unhappiness in his soul, it seeming to him that he had failed to do his duty, and aroused his indignation against the Moor, it seeming to him that he had done wrong in allowing a Moor to say such things about Our Lady, and to be obliged to defend her honor. And thus he was overcome by the desire to go in search of the Moor and to run him through with his sword for what he had said; and persisting much in the struggle of these desires, in the end he remained in doubt, not knowing what he was bound to do. The Moor, who had preceded him, had said he was going to a place a little farther ahead on the same road, very close to the main road, but through which the main road did not pass.

"And then, tired of examining what was the best thing to do, not finding any certain way of resolving it, he decided thus, namely that he would give the mule free rein as far as the point where the roads divided;

and if the mule took the road for the village, he would go in search of the Moor and would stab him; and if it did not go toward the village but took the main road, he would let him be. He did as he had thought, and Our Lord determined that though the village was little more than thirty or forty paces away and the road leading there was wider and better, the mule took the main road and left the road to the village."

After this episode, Saint Ignatius moves straight on without comment. But we know today that this scene of indecision between two roads, one that would have led him to assassinate an unknown Moor, the other that led Saint Ignatius to Montserrat and to all the rest of his life, is a marvelously vivid image of this *śraddhā*, this trust in some relationship between the mind and the world that touches the life of all of us at every moment. By which I mean: of all of us without distinction, whether or not we belong to a religious denomination. Having arrived at this point, it ought to be clear that religion, understood in this way through its two imperative terms, *knowledge* and *faith* (*śraddhā*), affects every aspect of our experience. In every aspect of our experience we are in contact with things that escape the control of our ego—and it is precisely in the area outside our control where we find that which is most important and essential to us. This, in the end, is the reason why the books I have mentioned so far have been published by Adelphi. Associated with these books—sometimes juxtaposed, sometimes overlaying them—are works of mythology that, as Father Pozzi observed, are "not perfectly synonymous." Here again there is a relationship with the unknown. If everywhere—in the forests of Brazil and the Kalahari Desert, in ancient China and Homer's Greece, in Mesopotamia and Egypt just as in Vedic India—the first form in which language manifested itself was the story, and a story that each time told of beings that were not entirely human, then this presupposes that no other use of words appeared to be more effective in establishing contact with entities that are around us and beyond us. And there is no risk of these stories, often immensely remote in time and space, being extraneous or inaccessible to us. All mythical stories, whatever their origin, are to do with something very close to us, though we often fail to realize it. And there's no better way of showing this than with another story, this time Hasidic, told by Martin Buber and again by Heinrich Zimmer:

"Rabbi Eisik, son of Rabbi Jekel, lived in the ghetto of Cracow. He had remained unbroken in his faith through years of affliction and was a pious servant of the Lord his God.

"One night, as this pious and faithful Rabbi Eisik slept, he had a dream; the dream enjoined him to proceed afar, to the Bohemian capital, Prague, where he should discover a hidden treasure, buried beneath the principal bridge leading to the castle of the Bohemian kings. The rabbi was surprised, and put off his going. But the dream recurred twice again. After the third call, he bravely girded his loins and set forth on the quest.

"Arriving at the city of his destiny, Rabbi Eisik discovered sentries at the bridge, and these guarded it day and night, so that he did not venture to dig. He only returned every morning and loitered around until dusk, looking at the bridge, watching the sentries, studying unostentatiously the masonry and the soil. At length, the captain of the guards, struck by the old man's persistence, approached, and gently inquired whether he had lost something or perhaps was waiting for someone to arrive. Rabbi Eisik recounted, simply and confidently, the dream that he had had, and the officer stood back and laughed.

" 'Really, you poor fellow!' the captain said. 'Have you worn your shoes out wandering all this way only because of a dream? What sensible person would trust a dream? Why look, if I had been one to go trusting dreams, I should this very minute be doing just the opposite. I should have made just such a pilgrimage as this silly one of yours, only in the opposite direction, but no doubt with the same result. Let me tell you my dream.'

"He was a sympathetic officer, for all of his fierce mustache, and the Rabbi felt his heart warm to him. 'I dreamt of a voice,' said the Bohemian, Christian officer of the guard, 'and it spoke to me of Cracow, commanding me to go thither and to search there for a great treasure in the house of a Jewish rabbi whose name would be Eisik son of Jekel. The treasure was to have been discovered buried in the dirty corner behind the stove. Eisik son of Jekel!' the captain laughed again, with brilliant eyes. 'Fancy going to Cracow and pulling down the walls of every house in the ghetto, where half of the men are called Eisik and the other half Jekel! Eisik son of Jekel, indeed!' And he laughed, and he laughed again at the wonderful joke.

"The unostentatious Rabbi listened eagerly, and then, having bowed deeply and thanked his stranger-friend, he hurried straightway back to his distant home, dug in the neglected corner of his house and discovered the treasure which put an end to his misery. With a portion of the money he erected a prayer-house that bears his name to this day."

What is the point—or at least the first point—of this wonderful story? Certainly not that the real treasure is always right there beside us. This would seem too much of a reassuring commonplace. The treasure beside us, in itself, is inert, as though it didn't exist. The real point is the journey, or rather: the improbable journey. An improbable journey because it leads far away, to an unlikely place—and above all a journey that relies, through an act of *śraddhā*, upon something that by definition is elusive and gives no guarantee: upon a dream. But it is the journey alone that makes the treasure exist. And that should be enough of an answer to the question about the usefulness of mythologies. The first virtue of stories, after all, is plainness, an evidence that speaks for itself, from the fabric of the story itself. A good publisher is one who publishes one tenth of the books that he would like to, and perhaps ought to, publish. The religious and mythological works in the Adelphi catalog should therefore be seen as indicating a path along which actual books are accompanied in every direction by many virtual books, like friendly shadows. And I would like to add that a good publisher is also someone in whose books these friendly shadows are naturally and irresistibly brought to life. They communicate to us from remote places, from spaces that are still boundless, waiting once more to be evoked, in the usual form of pages to be read.

A LETTER TO A STRANGER

The cover flap is a humble and arduous literary form for which there is as yet no theorist or historian. For a publisher, it is often the only opportunity to spell out what spurred him to choose a particular book. For the reader, it is a text to be read with caution, for fear of it being a piece of surreptitious hype. And yet the cover flap is part of the book, of its physiognomy, like the color and picture on the front cover, like the typeface in which it is printed. And a literary civilization can be recognized by the way its books are presented.

The history of the book had traveled a long and tortuous path before the appearance of the cover flap. Its noble forebear is the dedicatory epistle, another literary genre that flourished from the sixteenth century, where the author (or printer) addressed the prince who had given his patronage to the work—a genre no less awkward than the cover flap, since here the purpose was flattery rather than commercial enticement. Despite this, so often and in so many books, the author (or the printer) allowed the truth—and even drops of his poison—to emerge between the lines of the opening dedication. The fact remains, however, that as soon as the book comes into existence, the cover flap seems inevitably to be regarded as a form that kindles mistrust.

In modern times there is no longer a prince to address, but a *public*. Will this perhaps have a clearer and more recognizable face? Anyone who thinks so is mistaken. For some, it could even be the mistake on which their very profession is founded. But the story of publishing, when looked at closely, is a story of endless surprises, a story where uncertainty reigns. The whim of the prince is replaced by another, more pervasive and no less powerful whim. And the possibilities for misunderstanding are multiplied. Let's start with the word *public*: those who talk about a *public* generally think of a large and amorphous entity. But reading is solitary, like thought—and it presupposes the obscure and lone choice of a single person. The whim implicit in the choice of the patron who offers support to a writer (or printer) is, after all, better founded and therefore less of a whim than that of an unknown reader confronting a work or an author about which he knows nothing.

We watch a reader in a bookshop: he picks up a book, leafs through it—and for a short instant he is entirely cut off from the world. He is listening to someone speaking, whom others cannot hear. He gathers random fragments of phrases. He shuts the book, looks at the cover. Then he often takes a brief glance at the cover flap, hoping for some assistance. At that moment, without realizing it, he is opening an envelope: those few lines, external to the text of the book, are like a letter written to a stranger.

For many years, once Adelphi had begun publishing, we found ourselves asking the question: "What is the policy of the publishing house?" It was a question that was colored by a certain moment in time when the word *policy* was synonymous with *politics*, which found its way into everything, even the choice of coffee at a bar. Yet the question, despite its awkwardness, was right. Over the past century the figure of the publisher has faded further and further into the background. He has become an invisible minister who dispenses words and images in accordance with criteria that are not immediately apparent, and which stir universal curiosity. Does he publish to make money, like so many other producers of goods? Deep down, few believe this, due, if nothing else, to the fragility of the profession and the market. There is an immediate doubt, in this case, whether money is sufficient to justify everything. Something *extra* is always attributed to the publisher. If there ever was a publisher who published *only* to make money (and I have never met one), no one would take any notice of him. And he would probably go out of business fast, confirming the opinions of the skeptics.

In the early years, one was struck by a certain *lack of*

connection between Adelphi books. Appearing one after
the other in the same Biblioteca series were a fantasy
novel, a Japanese treatise on the art of theater, a popular
book on animal behavior, a Tibetan religious text, and
an account of imprisonment during the Second World
War. What bound all of these together? Paradoxically,
after a number of years, any concern about a lack of connection was reversed into quite the opposite: the recognition of a clear connection. In several bookshops, where
the shelves are divided by subject matter, I have found—
alongside labels for Cookery, Economics, History, etc.—
another label in the same graphics, that simply said
"Adelphi." This peculiar reversal that various booksellers
and many readers had come to notice was not unwar-
ranted. A publishing house can be set up for a whole
variety of reasons, and according to a whole variety of
criteria. What seems most normal for a large publishing
house today could be described as follows: to publish
books that each relate to one section of this vast entity
that is the public. There will therefore be coarse books
for coarse people and exquisite books for exquisite
people, in proportion to the size attributed to each of
those sections.

But an editorial program can also be built up according to quite the opposite criterion. What is a publishing house other than a long, serpentine progression
of pages? Each segment of that serpent is one book. But
what happens if we look upon that series of segments
as a single book? A book that contains within it many
genres, many styles, many periods, but which proceeds

continually and naturally, always in the expectation of one new chapter, which each time is another author. A perverse and polymorphous book that aims toward *poikilía*, "variegation," without shrinking from contrast and contradiction, but where even rival authors develop a subtle complicity that perhaps they had failed to see in their lifetime. After all, this strange process by which a series of books can be read as a single book has already happened in the mind of somebody, or at least in the mind of that anomalous entity behind each individual book: the publisher.

This view produces various consequences. If a book is primarily a *form*, then a book comprising a sequence of hundreds (or thousands) of books will also be, first and foremost, a form. In a publishing house of the kind I am describing, a *wrong* book is like a wrong chapter in a novel, a weak point in an essay, a jarring splash of color in a painting. To criticize the publishing house would thus be rather like criticizing an author. Such a publishing house could be compared with an author whose writing consists only of centos. But weren't the first Chinese classics all centos?

I don't wish, though, to be misunderstood: I don't expect any publisher to become like a Chinese classic. It would be dangerous for his mental stability, which is already threatened by so many pitfalls and temptations. Not least of these—and destined for a promising future—is the temptation that is the perfect mirror opposite of what we might call the *temptation of the classical Chinese text*. By this I mean the possibility of becoming the character Adolf Loos called the "poor little rich man," who wanted to live in an apartment designed by his architect down to the tiniest detail, and in the end felt completely alien and shamed in his own home. The architect complained that he had dared to wear a pair of slippers (also designed by the architect) in the living room and not in the bedroom.

No, my proposal is that there should always be one minimum but essential requirement incumbent on publishers. And what is this indispensable minimum? That the publisher enjoys reading the books he publishes. But isn't it perhaps true that all books that have given us some pleasure become a composite creature in our minds, whose constituent parts are linked by an irresistible affinity? This creature, formed by chance and by persistent study, could become the model for a publishing house. And, for example, for one whose very name—Adelphi—reveals a propensity for affinity.

All of this has left its mark on the cover flaps I have written (1,089 up to now). From the very beginning, they obeyed one single rule: that we ourselves could take them at face value; and one single desire: that our readers, contrary to custom, could do the same. In that cramped rhetorical space, less fascinating than that of a sonnet but equally exacting, there was room for just a few effectual words, like when you introduce one friend to another and you must overcome the slight embarrassment that always exists in every introduction, above all between friends, as much as respecting the rules of good manners that prevent you from emphasizing the defects of the friend being introduced. But there was, in all this, also an element of constraint: it is well known that the art of sound praise is no less difficult than that of scathing criticism. And it is also well known that the number of adjectives appropriate for praising writers is far less than the number of adjectives available for praising Allah. Repetition and limitation are part of our nature. After all, we will never manage to greatly vary the movements we carry out when getting out of a bed.

III

GIULIO EINAUDI

Publishing is a profession in which very few achieve true excellence. If we look around the world and at the whole of the past century, there have been many good publishers (meaning: those who have published good books). Many able publishers as well (meaning: capable of publishing books of every kind). But few great publishers. Certainly many fewer than the great writers they themselves have published. Giulio Einaudi was one of those few great publishers.

How do we gauge the greatness of a publisher? The question doesn't seem to have stirred many minds. There's no point looking in the histories of publishing, which at best offer a certain amount of useful data and information on various aspects of that activity. But they don't even try to give a judgment about quality, which ought to be as clear-cut and detailed as the judgment of a sonnet or an epic poem. It is best then to go back to the beginning, since a form is sometimes expressed to its fullest potential in its earliest moments. This happened, for example, in the history of photography. Anyone wanting to know what photography can be should begin by studying Nadar. But who was the Nadar of publishing? A Venetian publisher, Aldus Manutius. He was the first to see publishing as a form. A form in every respect: above all, of course, for the choice and sequence of published titles. Then for the texts that go with them (the opening pages that Aldus himself wrote are the noble ancestors not only of all modern introductions and afterwords but also of the cover flaps and editorial presentations, as well as publicity material). Then for the print form of the book and its qualities as an object. And here it is well known that Aldus was the unparalleled master: many agree that the most beautiful book ever printed is his *Hypnerotomachia Poliphili* (which appeared in 1499 as a rather difficult novel by an obscure living author: another sign of the publisher's excellence is not just in publishing established classics but devoting just as much care to an unknown new writer). It will be said that the *Hypnerotomachia* was a unique creation, unrepeatable in every sense. But we also have to thank Aldus for the invention that was to have the most sensational fortune and is reproduced every day millions of times over. He invented the paperback: it was his *Sophocles* of 1502. For the first time a book appeared in a format and with a page layout that could easily be reproduced by a publisher of today, five hundred years later. I am fortunate enough to own a copy of that *Sophocles* and know that I could slip it into my jacket pocket at any time, go and sit in a café, and read his *Philoctetes*. One final observation: the form of a publishing house can also be seen in the way in which its various books *go together* (the texts as well as the volumes in their physical appearance), in the same way that chapter twenty-three and chapter eighty of a vast novel by Dumas go together or the third and the ninth distich of an elegy by Propertius.

Publishing as *form*, which is the supreme form of publishing, therefore began in Italy, in Venice, in the twenty years around the beginning of the sixteenth century. But brilliant discoveries can also be forgotten and buried. Aldus's passage was like that of a meteor—and he certainly left little mark on the turbulent book trade over the next centuries. And so publishing generally became a very chancy business with not much profit (exactly as it is today), fascinating in every aspect but lacking in that formal excellence and rigor that Aldus first displayed.

Let us move straight on to Italy in the 1930s. Roberto Bazlen used to say that a country's publishers are to be judged by browsing in its secondhand bookstalls. And he once taught us the difference, in a few memorable lines on Trieste immediately after the First World War, between modern publishing in the German language and Italian publishing: "You should have seen the libraries that ended up on bookstalls in the ghetto, straight after the war, when Austria was in ruins and the Germans were leaving or selling off the books of people killed during the war. A whole great unofficial culture, books that were truly important and completely unknown, lovingly sought and collected by people who read that book because they needed to have that very book. All stuff that passed through my hands, where I discovered stuff I had never expected to come across, but most of it, whose importance I hadn't yet understood, slipped by me. Even now, if I hear of books that are totally unobtainable and have been reevaluated over these last twenty or thirty years, and which I'll never find again, I remember how they passed through my hands, on the bookstalls of the ghetto, thirty or so years ago, covered in dust and ready to be sold off at a lira each, at two lire each. I'm talking about the libraries of Germans, of Austrian naval officers, etc., but if the situation had been the other way around and if it had been the Italians that had gone, the bookstalls would have collapsed under the weight of Carducci, Pascoli, D'Annunzio, and Sem Benelli, backed up by Zambini and other wretched folk."

That Italy in which fascism, as we know, banned a certain amount of books but let many others pass through (and above all would have allowed them through if someone had wanted to publish them) was where Giulio Einaudi grew up, in a family belonging to the intellectual elite that Elena Croce so well described in *Lo snobismo liberale*. The young Einaudi wasn't, and would never be, a reader. He didn't have, and would never have, a deep understanding of any particular field. But through a natural gift, he could make good use of one of the peculiar characteristics of that strange elite into which he was born: to search out and recognize people "of worth" (as they used to say at that time). He also had an innate elegance, a sense of the invincible magic that aesthetic appearance can have (I cannot forget how Gianfranco Contini, the great critic and philologist, one day presented his collection *Varianti* at the Seeber bookshop in Florence and, leafing through the volume with delight, described it as "delicate to the touch"). So Giulio Einaudi started up a publishing house that very soon stood out above all the others as a creature with a different physiology. Not that Italy at the time was a publishing desert. The books that Benedetto Croce suggested to Laterza were of a high level, the early books of the Medusa series, published by Mondadori, were of excellent quality, La Nuova Italia's Il Pensiero Storico collection offered essential works by eminent scholars including Mikhail Rostovtzeff, Walter F. Otto, Werner Jaeger, and Julius von Schlosser, some of which still await translation in other countries. But the overall sight of an Italian bookstall during that period must have been depressing, a picture of rare intellectual and physical drabness. The real Europe was elsewhere. And real Italian readers looked out, each month, for the latest publications by Gallimard rather than those of Italian publishers.

Giulio Einaudi probably began publishing as such without knowing it, driven by an exacting and radical sense of vocation. But in the years immediately after

the Second World War his distinctive qualities must
have already been very clear, even if he would certainly
have described them in another way. It was then, in
fact, that he must have been struck by the image of the
publisher as Supreme Pedagogue or as a Sovereign who,
in accordance with his enlightened designs, selects the
matter that makes culture so that, little by little, it is
octroyée, granted, to the people. It was certainly a splendid
opportunity. After twenty years of fascism, everything
seemingly had to be done or redone. The Christian
Democrats, on the other hand, with their flaccid and
obstinate shrewdness, had let it be known that all they
wanted was the plain, mute, perpetual management of
political and economic power. They could leave culture
to be administered by the Left—after all, they were not
cut out to deal with it, nor did it even attract them.
They even abandoned cinema to its own devices, content to keep an eye on necklines. But they were in no
doubt when television appeared—that was certainly
for them.

Giulio Einaudi understood all this better than anyone
else. If it's true that every publisher tends inevitably to
be something of an autocrat and something of a Don
Juan (which was Erich Linder's definition, and he knew
every publisher), it can be said that Italy in the immediate postwar years was like a *hortus deliciarum*. In the case
of Giulio Einaudi, the autocrat regarded it as his natural

task to educate and drill the whole population of the Left, identifiable above all in the numerous ranks of teachers, from primary school to university, who would contribute much to the fortunes of the publishing house, though padding out the catalog with too many of their own books. As for the Don Juans, there were hundreds of authors whom no one had previously approached or had known how to handle properly, all waiting to be seduced by him. And sometimes there were opportunities to acquire whole *corps de ballet*: the Polish historians, Russian semiologists . . . And so, after the death of Benedetto Croce and up to the end of the 1980s, Giulio Einaudi was the man with the most influence over Italian cultural life. In the ostentatious display of lay piety following his death, I don't think anyone made this elementary observation. And so one day, as a legitimate reaction, someone spoke of Einaudi's "dictatorship" and "hegemony." Clumsy and inappropriate words. There was no sign of pistols drawn. And Italy, in any event, had plenty of eccentrics who wouldn't have been intimidated by any kind of "hegemony." I think it was more of a tacit domination and subtle hypnosis. The spontaneous zeal of Italian subjects was much greater than the *libido dominandi* to be found inside the publishing house. Oddly connected with all this was the strange phenomenon to be seen at commemorations: pious elegies to Giulio Einaudi were often counterbalanced by the list of his supposed defects: above all capriciousness, the ability to set collaborators against

each other, a certain dandyism, insolence, inherent arrogance, a certain recklessness. Yet I think it was these
very characteristics that enabled the publishing house
to maintain its charm for so long. Those who worked
with Giulio Einaudi were of every kind: some truly remarkable (and only rarely or sporadically listened to),
others surly and above all tone deaf to quality. If some
of them had been freely able to publish their favorite
books, I think the overall result would have been fairly
abysmal. And the form of the publishing house would
certainly have suffered. But wasn't it Giulio Einaudi himself who spoke of the publishing house as being a "collective" where "joint decisions" are made, as a "research
laboratory," as a workshop that constantly produces
"work tools," or even as a "public service"? Yes, but these
were typically reassuring words for the profane—and it
is well known that the solicitous educators of the masses
never want to upset the ignorant too much (and perhaps they themselves end up believing the glib words
they repeat at every conference or interview). Day-to-day
publishing practice was fortunately very different: in the
end, the only person capable of accurately divining what
was, and what was not, "an Einaudi book" was Giulio
Einaudi himself. This last, secret process through which
a book had to pass before being published by Einaudi
could certainly lead to enormous and repeated errors
in judgment. But paradoxically this further helped in
some way in giving the publishing house a more distinctive profile—an observation that is still relevant

today, at a time when publishing houses, especially the larger ones, seem to be like formless stockpiles where you can find everything, with a particular emphasis on the worst.

My intention was to pay homage to a great publisher, who in his heyday had perhaps only one equal in the world: Peter Suhrkamp. And I don't want to say here what I feel was missing in his catalog. I can only point out that what was missing was for me a vast part of the essential. But the question would be too long and complex. It would require a short book of its own. And this itself indicates how important Einaudi was, even for anyone who might find themselves radically opposed to him. In this respect, I would like to end with a brief story. Perhaps the moment of wildest (and altogether most disastrous) ambition for Einaudi was the encyclopedia venture. When the first volume appeared, I remember a friend of mine saying: "This is the last monument to Sovietism." And I think he was right. Not because the texts published were at all Soviet in themselves (they were far from it, and went in quite different and sophisticated directions), but because the pretension, implicit in the work, was Soviet in offering the correct version of how we ought to be thinking (though obviously presenting itself in a way that was multidimensional, meta-disciplinary, variegated, problematic, transversal, as the fashion of the time required).

But now I come to my brief story: one of the editors of the *Enciclopedia Einaudi* invited me one day to write the entry for "body." I told him I felt honored and per-plexed, and instinctively asked him who was going to be writing the entry for "soul." "There's no plan for such an entry," he immediately replied, as though I had asked something improper. At that moment I realized we would never have seen eye to eye.

LUCIANO FOÀ

Ihave been wondering whether I have ever known anyone so difficult to describe as Luciano Foà. After much thought I've come to the conclusion that there is no one who quite matches him. Though impeccably amiable, Foà was intensely saturnine in the way he related to others as well as in his own way of presenting himself. Also physically, he resembled an Egyptian scribe, crouched with his tablet between his legs, gazing fixedly in front of him. Like the scribe, he knew his task was to transmit with maximum precision something memorable, whether a list of provisions or a ritual text. No more, no less. He was interested only in getting to the bottom, touching the bedrock (if there was one) of people and things, getting there by probing slowly, cautiously, persistently. And he revealed himself in the same way, gradually and layer by layer. It took some time for me, who knew him when I was twenty-one and at the height of my youthful insolence, to recognize this last peculiarity. But its discovery, once it had dawned on me, gave me an enormous sense of relief and peace of mind.

In more than forty years, I never heard Foà resort to bombast or strong language. Whatever was going on outside the door of the room where we were talking—and I reckon, over the years, we must have spent thousands of hours in this way—I knew with complete certainty that Foà would never be caught up in it. And there were plenty of opportunities—political, literary, religious, editorial, psychological—almost every day during certain times and especially, I would say, in the 1960s and '70s, which were the most risky and also the most exciting years for us. His decade spent with Einaudi had been of fundamental importance for Luciano and I think he got the best from that place that it could give. But this period of his life also enabled him to determine once and for all what he *didn't* want and *didn't* like. Adelphi, from the very beginning, had to be something radically different. Between us we never felt the need to talk about a "project," "institutions," "programs," or "guidelines"—nor even "editorial policy." Our agreement was based on a tacit understanding, a kind of subterranean lake that fed our thinking and choices. We spoke, though never at length, about the way the wind was then blowing, before returning to what most interested us both: sorting out some detail about a book to be published. The golden rule that Foà always applied was that in a publishing house, as in a book, nothing is irrelevant, nothing is unworthy of full consideration. If many readers have found in Adelphi books a surplus of something that elsewhere can be entirely lacking, I think it is primarily this, which can be linked to Simone Weil's definition of *culture*: "Education of attention." I don't know of any definition of this word that is so short and so convincing.

The clearest memory I have of Foà in Adelphi's first office, in Via Morigi in Milan, is of a spacious, quiet room where he was sitting at a table—someone happy to be doing what he was doing. At that time Luciano was rereading and editing the already excellent translation of Georg Büchner's plays that Giorgio Dolfini had prepared for Adelphi. I remember that we discussed at length a point in *Leonce and Lena* about kisses that "*phantasieren*" on the lips of a young girl. These were the very early days of Adelphi and I was raring to get a number of things going. But that day I was also taught to understand the vital importance of that invisible scrutiny given to every word of a book that would soon be published.

Luciano did not have that omnivorous curiosity that may seem essential in the publishing world. He admired few writers and knew it would be very difficult to add, over the years, any others that were as close to his heart. In his view, and for his taste, there was only one constellation, whose stars were Stendhal, Kafka, Goethe, Joseph Roth, and Robert Walser. He also obviously admired many other authors. But among these writers, and a few others in his secret constellation, there was for him something akin to the difference he felt between

Roberto Bazlen's approach to life and that of many other figures of varied importance and interest that he had met. His clear choice was in favor of Bazlen, Roth, Walser.

Foà was always prepared to understand and to look for common ground in everyday life. He was just as affectionate toward a wide variety of people, whom he greatly admired, such as Giorgio Colli or Sergio Solmi or Mazzino Montinari. And a solid friendship bound him to such disparate people as Erich Linder or Silvio Leonardi or Alberto Zevi, who would remain closely associated with Adelphi and with Luciano himself until the end.

Foà's greatness was apparent above all at that most difficult moment of decision-making. He could be mistrustful or even impatient in his approach to certain remarkable books and people, but never once in over forty years did I witness him being won over by anything or anyone insubstantial. He had an outstanding ability to notice the false notes of people and things— those notes that we so often encounter. We owe an immense debt of gratitude to him for having exercised this mastery. If I ask what gave him that unflinching farsightedness of judgment—and here I mean above all in his negative judgment, since before arriving at a positive conclusion Foà always left his options open and played for time—and if I ask what aspect of his highly delicate personal equilibrium it related to, I think I couldn't but refer to what was perhaps Foà's secret and almost obsessive concern: *grace*, in the theological sense of the word, which then incorporates every other meaning. When we went out or met in the evening—often with his much loved and generous wife, Mimmina, who cheered his life, and sometimes with a few friends, who tended always to be the same—on countless occasions I saw the moment arrive when Luciano, irrespective of the matters we might have been discussing that evening, would focus attention on that word *grace*, unusual in any conversation. It was more important to him than any other word—more than ideas, more than talent or even genius. The true, decisive, and infinitely obscure distinguishing factor lay in being, or not being, touched by grace. This was the only fragment from any theology that struck him deeply. This way of thinking, in its impenetrable singularity, should be enough to understand how Foà stood out, alone, in the world in which he had grown up and in which he took part with every fiber. This ought to be enough to let us understand what a rare and enlightened being has died with him. May his memory remain and transmit to us something of that wise passion that Foà devoted to Adelphi.

ROGER STRAUS

It's easy to imagine all of us, over dinner at the Frankfurt Book Fair, sharing reasons for our gratitude to Roger. Reasons presumably personal and perhaps secret, about which I'll say nothing. But I'd like to offer a few words about one particular reason we certainly all feel grateful to him. Roger, in fact, more than anyone else, helped us to solve a mystery that is contained in the following question: why is publishing so pleasurable? I certainly don't want to suggest that this is a question of general interest. In fact, I doubt there are many in the outside world who ask it. Indeed, some would think that only a person who is in some way disturbed could ask a question like that. And yet such people exist and, consciously or unconsciously, are obsessed by that question. But who? Publishers themselves. Why, in fact, does anyone become a publisher? Certainly not for money, as the history of publishing amply demonstrates; and certainly not for the enjoyment of power, since any power the publisher has can only be fleeting and elusive, often insufficient to last more than a season. And I hope that no one is thinking of the word *culture*, since good manners require that it should not be mentioned, at least among educated people.

So what is left, apart from simple pleasure? We might not think it, looking at the expression on the faces of many of our colleagues here at Frankfurt. But anyone who had anything to do with Roger was compelled to believe it. Five minutes with him was enough to understand that there must be something wrong if the publisher's work is not frequently interspersed with laughter. And so, if our life as a publisher fails to offer sufficient opportunities for laughter, this means it's just not serious enough. And Roger was a very serious publisher. For Roger, books, authors, and publishers were all linked by a golden chain of stories. And a laugh or a smile now and again is a good sign when we find ourselves in the midst of a sequence of stories, if only as a counterpoint to the stories themselves, which can tend to be rather gloomy. And so the life of one publisher would contribute to this chain with a wealth of oral stories, which obviously run the risk of being lost if ever this chain is broken. In Roger's case we know we have nothing to fear, since the key to his trove of stories is in the safe hands of a single person: Peggy Miller. And I'm sure Jonathan

Galassi will keep up this tradition no less than the publishing house's many others. Roger was the fascinating, stern, and reassuring custodian of these stories, similar to one of those magnificent Indian chiefs portrayed by George Catlin, in which Baudelaire had recognized the archetypes of the dandy. Something of this kind came to mind when I saw him at his office desk or at his stand here at Frankfurt or with a martini before him at the Union Square Café. From his stories, which he used to recount with that irresistible drawl, we have all learned quite a number of valuable lessons we couldn't have been taught elsewhere. As publishers, we can hope for nothing better than to succeed in following that example, trying to be a part of the fun that Roger was able to spread throughout the publishing world for so many years. And if we have to stick to one rule, let it at least be the one that Joseph Brodsky—who, among other things, was one of the strongest links between us—once suggested as we were talking about Roger: "Whenever in doubt, he chooses the generous course."

When a publisher dies, his name generally appears in the newspapers followed by those of *his* authors, as if each of them were medals. In Roger's case, I'm sure that his best authors would be proud to see their names and the titles of their books followed by these simple words: "Published by Roger Straus."

PETER SUHRKAMP

Historians of today eagerly devote themselves to searching through materials that for many years had, quite wrongly, been ignored as legitimate sources of history: fashion and food, etiquette and agricultural equipment. But there are certain objects of study that seem more difficult to examine, perhaps since they are so obvious, vast, and unwieldy that they aren't even noticed.

One example: none of the many literary and cultural histories of the twentieth century have considered, except in passing, that flamboyant, many-headed, ruthless and refined form that the publisher and the publishing house have assumed over the past century. And yet a history of publishing over these last eighty years would be far more useful and revealing than those dull manuals that proceed by Movements and Manifestos, ecumenically jumbling the irrelevant with the essential, and tirelessly explaining that Expressionism was a cry, Surrealism was a dream, and Dadaism was the absurd.

Who is the publisher, in that peculiar physiognomy that began to take shape in the early years of the twentieth century? An intellectual and an adventurer, an industrialist and a despot, a bluffer and an invisible man, a visionary and a bookkeeper, a craftsman and a politician. The publisher is someone like Alfred Vallette, who claimed never to have read the books he published in the tiny rooms of Mercure de France, who said he only knew how to keep kitchen accounts, but his kitchen contained Alfred Jarry and Paul Léautaud, Marcel Schwob and Remy de Gourmont, Léon Bloy and Paul Valéry.

He is someone like Kurt Wolff—the "noble youth," as Karl Kraus called him—who in just a few years published new, or almost new, writers such as Franz Kafka, Gottfried Benn, Robert Walser, and Georg Trakl. He is someone like Gaston Gallimard, who started from the group that ran a literary journal that proudly snubbed its readership, and had a white front cover with a slim frame made of two red lines and a black line, and who ended up creating a sort of East India Company of the printed page.

Among this team, who were often far more adventurous than the characters in many of the novels they published, was Peter Suhrkamp: the last of a particular lineage and also the only one of them to have established a publishing house after the Second World War.

He came from an old family of farmers and craftsmen in the German north, and a strong element of craftsmanship always remained in his work, which for him was above all the art of "translating" a bundle of typewritten sheets into a book. Suhrkamp was a man whom no one, not even his closest friends and colleagues, ever claimed to know. Everyone had the impression, at a certain point, of coming up against something impenetrable, rock-hard, and melancholy. He came late to publishing—introduced to it by Bertolt Brecht. During Nazism, he managed incredibly to protect the most prestigious German publishing house, founded by Samuel Fischer in 1886, from every intrusion. But the growing resentment the Nazi leaders felt toward him finally exploded: he was imprisoned in a concentration camp and came out of it with his health ruined.

In 1950, at the age of fifty-nine, after many vicissitudes, he founded the publishing house that bears his name: Hermann Hesse and Brecht were, at that time, his two great authors: mutually incompatible, Suhrkamp was just as much a friend and admirer of each of them—and this already gives us an idea of the untranslatable peculiarity of his approach to life. Between 1950 and 1959, through hard work, often interrupted by long spells in clinics, he built up the clear outline of the new publishing house. Paradoxically, with a program that he described as elite, and without feeling any sense of guilt about it, Suhrkamp established the basis for the enormous worldwide success that several of his authors were to have in later times: not only Brecht and Hesse, but also Theodor Adorno, Walter Benjamin, and Ernst Bloch.

When the famous edition of Benjamin's writings appeared in 1955, edited by Adorno, Suhrkamp calmly wondered whether those two volumes would find a dozen true readers in Germany. In fact, in its first year, the bookshops sold 240 copies. Suhrkamp's farsightedness was also apparent in the choice of his successor, Siegfried Unseld: someone entirely different but who remained stubbornly loyal to the founder's original approach.

Thus, in twenty-five years, what George Steiner described as the "Suhrkamp culture" was formed, in which we find essentially the best of postwar German *critical* culture. Today is a difficult moment for that culture: the Frankfurt School, after the death of Adorno, survives only as a parody of itself, and the rare recent surprises in narrative have come from Austrian writers such as Thomas Bernhard, heirs of a tradition that is in many respects incompatible with Germany. But for those who might one day wish to find out about what happened in German culture over the second half of the twentieth century, through its times of misery and of greatness, the best guide is the catalog of the publishing house created by Peter Suhrkamp.

VLADIMIR DIMITRIJEVIĆ

I came to know Vladimir Dimitrijević at the Frankfurt Book Fair in the early 1970s. From time to
time we have all read scathing criticisms of that
place and that event, which is said to be the most terri-
ble example of the confusion of languages and of the
abasement of culture to commerce. I have never shared
these ideas. On the contrary, I rather enjoy the cha-
otic aspect of the fair, and the relationship between
money and the written word, between money and literature, seems to me at least worthy of interest. But the
main reason for defending the Frankfurt Book Fair,
the reason that, for me, counters any argument, is the
fact that there I came to know Vladimir Dimitrijević.
Until then I knew only one thing about Éditions L'Âge
d'Homme, namely that whenever an author from the
Slavic world came to my attention, I immediately noticed that he had been published or heralded by L'Âge

d'Homme. And I had heard that behind that name was a certain Monsieur Dimitrijević.

When I met him, I soon found something strange and rare: between us there was a certain fellow feeling, without our knowing why or of what nature. We began talking about books and that discussion never stopped. I think it all happened like this because we have a shared conviction: we both believe that by talking about books one enters a space that is much vaster, lighter, and freer than when one talks about the world or, worse still, about personal matters. Perhaps people become publishers just to endlessly prolong a conversation on books. When I read the thrilling pages of Dimitrijević's conversations with Jean-Louis Kuffer, where he speaks of his youth in Belgrade, I found that fever, that secret fervor that must nourish the immense patience of the publisher. During their conversations, Dimitrijević used two words to describe the job of the publisher: *ferryman* and *gardener*. Those two words, to an untutored ear, might seem like signs of modesty. On the contrary, I think they reveal the highest ambition. Both the ferryman and the gardener are involved in something that already exists: a garden to be cultivated or a traveler to be transported. But that thing usually called creation also involves something that preexists. Every writer possesses within him a garden to be cultivated and a traveler to be transported: nothing more. Otherwise, he would end up involved with something much less interesting: his own ego. But the two words used by Dimitrijević are not just an indication of the

highest ambition. For me they are also the manifesta-
tion of an ancient dream. I believe that unless someone
has an image of paradise it is very difficult to be a great
publisher. And a paradise—whatever form it takes—
will always be a garden with flowing water. This image
must, however, remain well hidden. And what I admire
in Dimitrijević is also the relationship between what is
hidden and what is visible. What is visible, in him, is
for example what I will call his *cult of the obstacle.* Dimitrijević practices the profession of publisher on the basis
of surmounting certain elementary obstacles such as
the difficulty in passing a manuscript from an office
desk to a printing press, from a printing press to a bookshop, from a bookshop to someone's mind. Dimitrijević has become an expert in all of these passages. And
for precisely this reason he has developed a metaphysics that is the foundation of his cult of the obstacle. I
would describe it as the metaphysics of the customs post.
With his small van, Dimitrijević is therefore the most
improbable and the most practical of publishers—and
what I find admirable is the very coexistence of these
two poles. All of this places him in a position of chronic
imbalance in relation to everything around us: an imbalance that Dimitrijević has sought and eventually
found. In fact, if we think of the authors and books that
Dimitrijević loves most and has published with the greatest passion, we immediately realize there is something
in these books that is too large or too small in relation
to what surrounds them: all have a certain boundless-
ness of soul. Those like Charles-Albert Cingria, like

Robert Walser, are perhaps too discreet to be noticed: perfect examples of those Swiss who—in the words of Dimitrijević—know how to "disappear without raising their voice." Or otherwise they are like Stanisław Witkiewicz or Aleksandr Zinovyev or Albert Caraco or Andrei Bely or Miloš Crnjanski: there is always something excessive about them, they overflow from the confines of reality. It is no coincidence that these authors, however different each is from the others, have found themselves under the same roof—that of Dimitrijević.

Every true publisher builds up, knowingly or otherwise, a single book consisting of all the books he publishes. Dimitrijević's book would be immense, possessed of a force that plays with form, held together by a total loyalty toward a tribe that no longer has a land to belong to, except for the pages of that same book. It is this, I believe, that creates the unity that gives form to a publishing house, it is this that has enabled Dimitrijević to encounter people who are essential to him and his publishing house, such as his wife, Geneviève, such as Claude Frochaux. From Belgrade to Lausanne, Dimitrijević carried out one of the longest journeys imaginable, an adventure impossible to measure, capable of being retold only by a latter-day Joseph Conrad. I often think of this when I find myself before other people in the publishing world whose adventures are also turning more into corporate sagas. And so, over the years, I have gradually understood the reasons that justified my original impression of Dimitrijević when we first met among the stands at the Frankfurt Book Fair—the impression that, on the one hand, there were those hundreds of publishers around us and, on the other, there was him, Dimitrijević, the ferryman, the barbarian, as he sometimes likes to call himself, the man who reached Switzerland with twelve dollars in his pocket and whose first question in English, since he still knew nothing of the French language, to a bookseller at the Librairie Payot in Lausanne, was: "Who is Amiel?" What Dimitrijević didn't say, but we know, is that the first good edition of Henri-Frédéric Amiel's *Journal intime* would be published a few years later by L'Âge d'Homme.

Thus I discovered that Dimitrijević's bracing imbalance was needed to balance the overly stable and rather dismal equilibrium of so many others. I hope, for him and for us all, that his bracing imbalance long continues.

IV

FAIRE PLAISIR

There is a keen paradox in the publishing world of today. On the one hand, everyone wants to be a publisher. If someone producing french fries was able to call himself a publisher, he'd do so straight away. There is still something inherently fateful and prestigious about the title, as if it were a higher role than that of a mere producer. On the other hand, there are those who claim ever more frequently and aggressively that the very role of the publisher is basically superfluous. They paint a future in which the publisher could become an atavism, a residual organ, the reason for which lies a few stages back in prehistory. The perpetual arguments on self-publishing are based on this perspective.

But how and when (after all, it was only recently) has this strange situation arisen? The world is experiencing a sort of infatuation with information technology that has now reached fever pitch. Its main article of faith is immediate access to everything. The tablet, or whatever other device, has to guarantee that everything is obtainable (literally, in that it can be summoned at a single touch). But not just that: it must also happen inside a minimum number of square centimeters. The device thus tends to become a two-dimensional shadow brain that has none of the mucilaginous consistency of the human brain.

In the face of such a splendid prospect, which grows wider and better every day, the publisher can only seem like a miserable obstacle, an intermediary whom no one feels they need any longer, since immediate availability is what everyone yearns for. *Immediacy*: that's the key word. In the same way that Rousseau's "general will" is something that should in the end render so many intermediate institutions useless (and sweep them away altogether, if possible, to avoid their evil influence), likewise information technology aims toward a situation—its own utopian vision—in which, as everything is connected with everything else, the result is an *ordo rerum* in which everyone can claim to have contributed. This would be a parody of that ancient world which was built on the network of *bandhus*, the "connections" to which the Vedic texts refer. It would be the fulfillment of what René Guénon foresaw under the name of "*contre-initiation*." Whether or not a world of this kind is desirable does not, for most people, seem a question of any urgency, so that it can just as well be diverted off to some talk show and abandoned there. Yet there's an urgency to move further ahead than ever before in the minia-

turization and multiplication of the functions of information technology, as if perpetual motion had become
the inverted image of the perfect immobility claimed
by the Egyptian priests when they told Herodotus that
for 11,340 years "the affairs of Egypt underwent no
change."

In this turbulent process, which surrounds us like
a *cloud of knowing*—once again an inverted image of the
cloud of unknowing, the title of the text by the great anonymous English mystical writer, which at the same time
uses a word much loved by the digital cult, the *cloud*—
is there some element that *is lost forever* or are we witnessing a process of expansion and intensification of
elements that already exist? The investigation could be
long, with results often inconclusive. But, if we limit the
field to that of publishing, it can be said with certainty
that there is one element that the *cloud of knowing* (or,
more accurately, the *cloud of information*, though hasn't
the very distinction between information and knowledge
become blurred?) can do without: *judgment*, that prime-
val capacity to say yes or no. But judgment was the basic
founding element for the existence of the publisher,
that strange producer who needs no factory and can
even reduce his administrative structure to a minimum.
Yet he has always had one undeniable prerogative: to
say yes or no to a manuscript and decide in what form
to present it. But if judgment can be easily dispensed
with, this is even truer of form. Indeed, discussion about
form could soon become meaningless. What's the point
of talking about book covers if these now exist only on

books that are *physical* (another term belonging to that involuntary metaphysics that is so often applied today)? And what can be said about a book cover other than it *sells* or *doesn't sell*? What then about a *series*, an obsolete notion? As for the *page*, not only is it limited to physical books, but it appears more and more as a neutral and standard element. And the text that accompanies the books? It generally consists of a heavy dose of praise, together with a modest combination of enticements whose effect obviously diminishes the more often they are used.

While all this is going on, how do good publishers continue to operate? It's sufficient to read the correspondence between Flaubert and the Goncourt brothers and their publisher Michel Lévy, from around 1860, to see that exactly the same things were discussed then between author and publisher as are discussed today: first of all contracts (where the publisher and the author alternately assume the role of thief), then proof errors, inadequate publicity, bookshop window displays, attempts to get certain reviews, slow production schedules, the prospect of an award (to be accepted or refused), and the chronic lethargy of the public. These features of the publishing physiology have remained more or less unaltered. The numbers and sizes have changed. Though not much. If Descartes's *Discours de la méthode* was published in 2,000 copies, an American university press of today might print it in 1,800 copies.

And it's pointless dreaming about high print runs, even in the larger markets. Today, if a book sells 10,000 copies, "the publisher is happy" (Sonny Mehta, in conversation). So what then is the substantial difference? Once again, judgment. The perception of a book's quality or lack of quality is increasingly becoming an evanescent and secondary element. Is that particular book OK or not? What else does it connect with? Is it *cool* or *uncool*? Is it trendy or out of date? Would it work as an e-book? Would the author travel or not? How would he look on television? These are questions that are seriously weighed. Discussing the ugliness—or beauty—of a book seems inappropriate, out of place. This happens inside the publishing houses because it also happens in the mind of the world at large. If a group of people who hardly know each other start talking about books, in whatever part of the globe, the discussion will immediately turn to the format— electronic or physical—of the books, to the economic prospects of publishing (about which everyone seems nobly concerned), to the best technology for reading the books themselves. Very rarely will the discussion dwell on a single book, on a single writer. While the cinema continues to produce a certain number of films each year that *everyone has to know about*, at least by word of mouth, the same is not true for books. Even passing from one country to another it will be apparent that the majority of most popular authors in a particular country are totally unknown in a neighboring country. As for quality, such an argument would be difficult to introduce. Too confusing. Knowledge of single books is often nonexistent. The conversation would eventually devolve into casual snatches of information. And very soon, to general relief, it would go back to discussion for or against electronic books.

What is left for the publisher to do? There is still a scattered tribe of people in search of something that may be called literature without qualification, of something that is thought, that investigates (here again without qualifications), that is gold and not tin, that doesn't have the flimsiness typical of recent years. *Faire plaisir* was Debussy's reply to someone who asked what was the purpose of music. The publisher might also seek to *faire plaisir* to that scattered tribe, offering a place and a form that can give them what they are looking for. A task that seems more difficult today, not for lack of resources, but because the field of vision is obscured by the mass of what becomes available every day. And the publisher himself knows that not many people would notice if he disappeared from the field altogether.

THE OBLITERATION
OF PUBLISHER IDENTITY

Anyone who tries writing a history of publishing in the twentieth century will encounter a fascinating, eventful, and complex story. Much more than what is to be found in publishing in the nineteenth century. And it was the very first decade of the twentieth century that produced the essential novelty: the idea of the publishing house as a *form*, as a highly singular place that would bring together works that were mutually congenial—even if at first sight they seemed divergent or even contrasting—and would publish them following a clearly defined style that was distinct from any other. This was the idea—never clearly expressed because it didn't seem necessary—around which several friends met up to establish two journals, *Die Insel* in Germany and *La Nouvelle Revue Française* in France. Later, alongside each journal, thanks to the efforts of Anton Kippenberg and Gaston Gallimard respectively, a new publishing house was established following the same lines. But the same idea, over the same period, would guide publishers as different as Kurt Wolff, Samuel Fischer, Ernst Rowohlt, Bruno Cassirer, and later on in other countries, Leonard and Virginia Woolf, Alfred Knopf, and James Laughlin, each in their own particular way and not necessarily linked to a journal. And finally Giulio Einaudi, Jérôme Lindon, Peter Suhrkamp, and Siegfried Unseld.

The first examples I mentioned were publishers who came from the wealthy educated bourgeoisie, who shared a certain taste and attitude of mind, who launched their enterprise out of sheer passion, with no illusion about making it financially lucrative. Making money producing books was, then as now, a dicey venture. With books, as everyone knows, it's very easy to lose money but difficult to make it—and even then they are modest sums, useful above all for continued investment. The industrial destinies of those firms varied greatly: some publishing houses, such as Kurt Wolff, closed after a few glorious years; others, such as Gallimard, are still prospering and firmly anchored in their origins. These publishing houses had each developed an unmistakably clear identity, defined not only in terms of the authors published and the style of their publications, but by the many occasions when those same publishing houses had been able to *say no* in terms of authors and style. And this is the point that brings us to today and to a contrary phenomenon that we are witnessing: I would call it *the obliteration of publisher identity*. If we compare the first decade of the 1900s with the one that has just passed, we immediately see two entirely opposite trends. In the first decade of the twentieth century the idea of the publishing house as a form was developed, an idea that then dominated the whole century, sometimes leaving a crucial mark on the culture of certain countries at certain times (as happened with the "Suhrkamp culture," as George Steiner described it when referring to Siegfried Unseld's Suhrkamp Verlag in 1960s and '70s Germany, or with Giulio Einaudi's Einaudi in Italy during the 1950s and '60s).

In the first ten years of the twenty-first century, however, we have witnessed a progressive blurring of differences among publishers. Today, as shrewder agents well know, everyone competes for the same books and those who win distinguish themselves only because, by winning, they have bought a title that will prove in the end to be a moneymaker or a disaster. Then, after a few months, whether it has been a success or a failure, the book in question is lost in the twilight of the backlist: a meager twilight that occupies an ever smaller and irrelevant space, much the same as the past itself occupies in the mind of the hypothetical book buyer whom the publisher is seeking to win over. All of this can be seen in the acquisitions lists and above all in the catalogs, those very significant bulletins through which books are presented to the booksellers—and which have now become so highly interchangeable in terms of their language, images (including photos of authors), and suggested selling points, and lastly in the physical appearance of the books. At this point it becomes seriously difficult for anyone to identify what a certain publishing house *cannot* do because it simply *isn't cut out for it*. It is noticeable that in the United States the name and logo of the publisher have become an increasingly discreet and at times almost imperceptible presence on book covers, as if the publisher didn't wish to seem too presumptuous. It will be argued that this is due to enormous structural changes that have taken place and are still going on in the book trade. An incontrovertible observation, to which it can be answered that such changes would not *in themselves* be incompatible with the continuation of that line of publishing as form, in the way I described earlier. In fact, one of the notions venerated today in whatever branch of industrial activity is that of the *brand*. But there can be no brand unless it is based on a clear, firm selectivity and idiosyncrasy of choice. Otherwise the power of the brand can never be elaborated and developed.

My fear is another: the drastic change in production conditions may have led many people to believe, wrongly, that a certain idea of publishing which was a characteristic of the twentieth century is now obsolete in the enlightened new millennium. A hasty and baseless judgment, even though it must be recognized that some time has elapsed since any publishing house inspired by those old and evergreen ideas has successfully emerged. Another distressing symptom is a certain failure to understand the quality and extent of a publisher's job. The summer of 2011 saw the death of two great figures of publishing: Vladimir Dimitrijević, publisher of L'Âge d'Homme, and Daniel Keel, publisher of Diogenes Verlag. Testimony to their work can be found in catalogs with thousands of titles that could happily keep an avid young reader going for years. But very little of this appeared in the newspapers reporting their deaths. It was said, for example, that Daniel Keel was a "friend to his authors," as if this characteristic were not an obvious requirement for any publisher— and inevitable, moreover, in the obituaries of certain editors who are well known for their devotion to their authors. But there's quite a difference between a publisher and an editor. A publisher is the person who shapes the profile of the publishing house. And he is judged and remembered, above all, by the virtues and defects of that profile. An even more embarrassing instance: the *Frankfurter Allgemeine* observed that Daniel Keel had created a third possibility between "serious literature" and "literature for entertainment." But for Keel the polestar of his literary taste was Anton Chekhov. Should we also include Chekhov in that no-man's-land that is not quite "serious literature" and yet goes beyond "literature for entertainment" (and in the case of Diogenes Verlag, it would have had to include writers such as Friedrich Dürrenmatt, Georges Simenon, and Carson McCullers)? The sad suspicion is that these judgments are an unwitting posthumous revenge for a successful slogan that Daniel Keel had one day invented: "Diogenes books are less boring." The unexceptionable assumption of that phrase is that, in the long run, only quality trumps boredom. But, if the perception of quality in everything that defines an object—whether it's a book or a publishing house—is ignored, since quality itself seems increasingly irrelevant, the road toward relentless monotony opens up, where the only thrill is provided by the electric shocks of high advances, large print runs, great publicity launches, and mega-sales—and just as often by large numbers of returned books, destined to fuel the flourishing pulping industry.

In the end, it seems clearer every day that, for information technology, the publisher is a hindrance, an intermediary who could happily be dispensed with. But the more serious suspicion is that publishers, at the moment, are collaborating with technology in such a way as to make themselves superfluous. If the publisher relinquishes his function as first reader and first interpreter of a work, it's hard to see why that work should accept a place in the framework of a publishing house. It's much better relying on an agent or distributor. The agent would then give a first judgment on the work, deciding whether or not to accept it. And the agent's judgment can obviously be more acute than what had, at one time, been the judgment of the publisher. But the agent neither has nor creates a *form*. An agent has only a list of clients. Otherwise one can also imagine an even simpler and more radical solution in which there is just the author and the (gigantic) bookseller who has brought together the functions of publisher, agent, distributor, and perhaps even commissioner.

The question arises whether this would mean a triumph for the democratic process or produce a general stultification. For my part, I tend toward the latter view. When Kurt Wolff, a century ago, published young prose writers and poets such as Franz Kafka, Robert Walser, Georg Trakl, and Gottfried Benn in his Der Jüngste Tag ("Judgment Day") series, those writers immediately found their first few readers because there was already something attractive about the appearance of those books, which looked like slim black exercise books with labels and came with no program announcements or publicity launches. But they suggested something that could already be sensed in the name of the series: they suggested a *judgment*, which is the real acid test for any publisher. In the absence of that test, the publisher might just as well withdraw from the scene without it hardly being noticed, and without causing too much regret. But then he'd have to find another job, since his brand value would be next to nothing.

ALDUS MANUTIUS'S
FLY SHEET

Five hundred years after its beginnings, the task of publishing has not yet managed to achieve a solid reputation. Part merchant, part circus impresario, the publisher has always been considered with a certain mistrust, like a clever huckster. And yet the past century may one day be considered the golden age of publishing. It would be futile to reconstruct French culture during the twentieth century without following the various events in the evolution of Éditions Gallimard; or if we examine a more restricted period, delving into the intellectual climate of the 1970s without referring to the hypnotic awe that emanated from Éditions du Seuil; in the same way that we would understand little about the German scene from the 1960s onward without considering the effects of the Frankfurt School, all of which was brought together in the publications of Suhrkamp; or we would know even less about Italian postwar culture if we ignored the highly educational role of Einaudi; or lastly, it would be strange to retrace the acrobatic transformation in Spain from the years of Franco to today without having at hand the chronological catalog of three publishers in Barcelona: Carlos Barral, Jorge Herralde, and Beatriz de Moura. In order to draw an outline of a culture, there is good reason to assess its publishing landscape well before its academic landscape, where the great scholars now live in a sort of enforced isolation, more or less content to do so according to the country, and the resources of individual universities.

But can we expect the golden age of the twentieth century to continue into the twenty-first century? Here the doubts are many and varied. The first of these relates to a certain way in which publishers now generally consider their work. In fact, the publishing trade shouldn't just be guarding against Google, but against itself, against its increasingly fainthearted conviction about its own necessity. Above all in Anglo-Saxon countries, which are the spearhead of publishing, given the predominance of the English language. For anyone entering a London or New York bookshop, it's increasingly difficult to recognize individual publishers on the New Books display. The name of the publisher is often discreetly reduced to one or two initials on the spine of the book. As for the book covers themselves, each are different—and in a certain sense too much the same. On each occasion they make a more or less successful attempt at packaging a text. And each has its own value, in obedience to the *one shot* principle. As for the authors, their books are brought together under the logo of one particular publishing house rather than another, primarily as a result of the negotiations between the author's agent and that particular publisher as well as personal contact between the author and a particular editor. The publishing house meanwhile tends to become an unnecessary link in the chain. There are, of course, notable differences of quality among publishing houses, but all within a spectrum in which there is the *highly commercial* (of the vulgar kind) at one extreme and the *highly literary* (of the soporific kind) at the other. Various names are to be found in a series of categories in the middle. Farrar, Straus and Giroux will be closer to the "literary" end and St. Martin's toward the "commercial" end, but without this implying any ulterior consideration, and above all without ruling out certain invasions of the pitch—the literary publisher may occasionally be tempted by the commercial title in the hope of replenishing his bank balance and the commercial publisher may always be tempted by a literary title, since aspiring to prestige is a weed that grows everywhere.

Most distressing about this distinction—which then corresponds to a certain mind-set—is the fact that it is false. It is clear that, in the spectrum I have just described, Simenon or his hypothetical modern reincarnation ought to be included in the highly commercial zone, and thus not eligible for any literary evaluation; and it is clear that many belonging to the pitiful category of "writers' writers" ought to be assigned automatically to the literary extreme. This works against the interests of both pleasure and literature. The true publisher—since such strange beings still exist—never reasons in terms of "literary" or "commercial" but, if anything, in the old terms of "good" and "bad" (and it is well known that the "good" can often be neglected or remain unrecognized). Above all, the true publisher is one who has the arrogance to claim that, in principle, none of his books will fall from the hands of any reader through tedium or an unassailable feeling of extraneousness.

About a century ago, some of the most important publishing houses of the twentieth century—Insel, Gallimard, and Mercure de France—were born or were taking their first steps. They had two features in common: they had been founded by a group of friends who were more or less affluent and marked by certain literary ambitions; and, before becoming publishing houses, they had been literary journals: *Die Insel*, *La Nouvelle Revue Française*, and *Mercure de France*. Then the figures who were to become the publishers—Anton Kippenberg, Gaston Gallimard, and Alfred Vallette—found their way with books. A similar experience would be unthinkable today since conditions have changed. Among other things, the category of literary journal no longer exists, or at least it has lost the subtle and discreet relevance it used to have. The only periodical to have retained its preeminence, its authority, and its relevance is *The New York Review of Books*, which, however, is first of all a journal of reviews and therefore doesn't

match the form that perhaps reached its peak of per-
fection around the 1930s with the twenty-nine issues of
Commerce, under the invisible and protective wing of
Marguerite Caetani.

If we ask what bound those small groups of friends
together in the early 1900s, the answer is found not in
what they wanted (often fairly vague and confused)
but in what they rejected. And it was a form of *taste* in
the sense in which Nietzsche used the word, as "in-
stinct of self-defense" ("Not to see, not to hear so many
things, not to let them near—first clear indication, first
proof that we are not chance, but a necessity"). This
passage to book publishing must indeed have been a
clever move if it proved so effective. Today, a hundred
years later and two generations on from its founder,
Gallimard is the leading publishing house in France
and is still recognizable for a certain "Gallimard taste"
which makes it possible to detect more or less whether
a book may or may not be a Gallimard title. Though
everything around has changed, the physiology of taste
that bound those small groups of friends together would
be an excellent antidote today in certain publishing
houses caught up in periodic concerns about their fad-
ing image or lack of identity. But at that point it would
also become apparent that taste is no longer, for the
most part, wrapped in that fabric of sensibility, which
has become a cloth rent with holes larger than the fabric
itself.

But this should not be dispiriting. It would certainly
be harder and less practicable to set up a publishing

house based on the enthusiasm of a small club of friends. But at the same time publishing—if it only wanted to, if it only had the courage—now has opportunities that at one time didn't exist. Over the last hundred years the area of what is *publishable* has vastly expanded, if we think only of the enormous quantity of anthropological, scientific, historical, and literary material that has accumulated over the twentieth century, just waiting to find a new form in publishing. Not just the Biblioteca series, but all Adelphi books from the very beginning, were based on this notion. It was an attempt to bring the most disparate texts and materials together in that broad, swirling current that carries with it all that a lively and agile mind can wish to read. Today, in fact, more than ever before, one of the prime objectives of publishing could be *to shift the line determining what is publishable* and include as feasible a lot of what currently lies outside that line. It would be an enormous challenge, not so different from the very beginning, when Manutius was working in Venice. This is perhaps the moment to recall what was the publisher's founding charter. It was a loose sheet of paper, printed by Manutius himself, that has survived by chance, glued into the binding of a copy of a Greek dictionary in the Vatican Library. Printed around 1502, that sheet of paper contained the text of a pact between scholars who were preparing editions of classical Greek texts for Aldus's publishing house. In the words of Anthony Grafton, "they agreed to speak only Greek in one another's company, to pay fines when they slipped, and to use the money (once enough had accumulated) to hold a symposium: a lavish common meal that was required to be better than the food usually distributed to Aldus's workers. Other 'philhellenes' would be admitted to the circle over time." We do not know today whether the rules of that New Academy of Aldus Manutius were ever applied. But it will be recalled that Luther's ninety-five theses and the *Déclaration des droits de l'homme et du citoyen* of August 26, 1789, were originally printed in the same way. Having said this, it is obvious that the tendency in the world and in publishing until now has been, and still is, to move in the opposite direction. And so the field of what is felt possible to do continues to shrink. "That would be very nice, but it's not possible" is a phrase frequently heard throughout the publishing world.

But if we go back to the early 1900s and to those publishers who had developed on the basis of an affinity among a small group of friends, it can easily be seen how many times those same publishers, with commendable recklessness, must have said at that time: "That would be very nice, let's try it." Otherwise it would be difficult to explain how for years Insel had published certain French editions in perfectly neat print (for example, Stendhal's *De l'amour*) in French for a German readership, or how in 1914, just as war was breaking out, the publisher Eugen Diederichs had dared to publish a monumental edition (first of all in terms of size) of the main Upaniṣads translated by Paul Deussen, a great Indologist and friend of Nietzsche. And those bold

enterprises certainly reduced neither Insel nor Diederichs to ruin, since a century later they remain two
important names in German publishing.

Projects of this kind would never succeed today.
Because publishers wouldn't have the imagination to
create them? Or because—some would argue—those
projects would be stopped immediately by sharp-eyed
publishing managers? Certainly, a century ago, the publishers I'm talking about didn't have managers but book-
keepers or accountants. And this probably made them
more ready and inclined toward risk. But there's something else. Over the course of the past hundred years,
the very physiognomy of the publisher has changed,
at least when we define him as someone who knows
the books he publishes and decides the form they
must have. If we accept this definition, there are very
few people today who can be given the title of *publisher*.
They could probably be counted on the fingers of two
hands. *Editors*, on the other hand, are many and increas-
ing, if *editors* are those who discover, follow, develop, and
launch a certain number of books within the catalog of
a publishing house. All *editors* are associated with a
list of authors and books as though they are *theirs*. This,
however, doesn't include the form itself—the catalog,
the program of the publishing house for which they
work. If a publishing house is not conceived as a form, as
a self-sufficient composition held together by a high
physiological compatibility between all of its constituent
parts, it easily turns into a casual association, incapable

of triggering that magical element—brand power—that even marketing experts consider essential for achieving some degree of success.

And here is the paradox faced by the publishing manager, who is a recent figure and now widespread throughout the book world: on the one hand he has been taught to extol the importance and the value of the brand, while on the other his approach can only weaken, and ultimately compromise, the special quality of the brand itself.

In his platonic form, the publishing manager feels he is the representative of a universal doctrine applicable to everything, without exception, and whose results are to be assessed, like every other branch of his doctrine, on the basis of figures that appear at the bottom of certain columns of figures. Those figures are the *bottom line*—and can be just as thrilling, depressing, mediocre, acceptable, in publishing as in button manufacturing or cosmetics, or with any other product or service for sale. Except that the publishing of books— those books that are not textbooks, that have no practical purpose, that appear in Italy under the unintentionally comic name of *various*—constitute one of the most frustrating and treacherous branches to which the manager's doctrine can apply. This seems to excite the representatives of this category even further, rather than deter them, almost as if they were horse breakers who want to show they can tame even the most high-spirited mounts. We are continually told of managers who moved into publishing from major industry. But there appear to be no cases of managers brought up in publishing who have gone into major industry. In publishing the manager arrives on the scene to be engulfed by it and disappear, or otherwise to remain there to the very end, producing more or less commendable results. But no manager has so far been associated with any memorable event in publishing. Nor is there ever any alternation of roles, any movement between one and the other, as happens in the rapport between politics and the academic and financial worlds, so that the academic temporarily *loaned* to politics returns to academic life, or the financier returns to Wall Street with a more substantial remuneration. The case of a manager who has made a fortune in publishing simply doesn't exist—or it must have been a modest fortune that hasn't been recorded in the annals. Whereas there have been several cases of managers from major industry who, after a swift dive into publishing, have made a hasty return to their own familiar territory just before causing irreparable damage (or else, more frequently, immediately after). How do we explain this reluctance of publishing to comply with a universal and hitherto unscathed doctrine such as that of management—or at least to provide it with satisfactory results? Here at last we must examine the peculiarities of this sector.

The size of the book trade is, above all, fairly modest, so that good results, obtained through hard work, will not produce sensational profits. It's much easier, however, to make large losses. Let's assume, for example, that the top manager of a publishing group orders his editors to snatch a group of bestselling authors from their rivals, attracting them through a large increase in their respective advances. And let's assume (as often happens) that all the new books by these authors are failures—or at least they produce revenues lower than the advances. At that point, all that remains is to pulp the hundreds of thousands of copies returned over the next few months, with a negative impact on next year's results. Nothing else. The bestselling author whose book doesn't reach the target at the first shot has almost no prospect of a second chance, as happens with certain books that can be gradually discovered or rediscovered or have unexpected luck in a discounted edition. As for books on current affairs, published in great haste because they deal with topics that *everyone* is talking about, they will soon be left behind by current affairs themselves, which soon require that everyone talks about something else. And what about publicity and commercial promotion? The costs of publicity and commercial promotion for an individual book become easily and manifestly disproportionate. A book is one of a hundred or two hundred or three hundred objects produced by the same firm and each is waiting (or, at least, their authors are each waiting) to get publicity, whereas a new perfume is a single object on which the whole promotional energy of a brand is concentrated. And the videos or photographs that go with a perfume are inevitably more captivating and memorable than press advertising for a novel. Kate Moss or Charlize Theron have never publicized a novel. For good reason. And a perfume can, in theory, be advertised in hundreds of airports throughout Asia, Europe, or the United States, whereas an Italian book is unlikely to be seen in more than a dozen medium-sized Italian airports. Among the great international successes of the last twenty years, there is no book whose success can be said to have been *forced* by publicity, whereas for many other kinds of products it can be said that the nature of the object was less important in its success than the publicity campaign that had launched it.

A new scenario seems, in all probability, to be appearing behind all this: a new publishing landscape populated by many editors, by even more publishing managers and marketing experts, but fewer and fewer publishers. I fear that many people wouldn't even be aware of such a radical change. Certain things disappear almost unnoticed. And sometimes they are things of fundamental importance. The question "Who has published this book?" could become less frequent because the answer would be irrelevant. Everything would move imperceptibly in the direction of the anonymous reader who once told me she never took any notice of who a book's publisher and author were. And what would happen in the end? There would still be good and bad books. But those good books would appear as sporadic, isolated events, with no congenial context into which to fit them. Otherwise, not much would change in the bookstalls. Apart from this: one figure would have vanished—namely, the publishing house, the concept of the publishing house and its form—whose vital role would be recognized by some people too late. The only comfort would then be in the thought that what seems most likely doesn't always happen. In other words, virtue isn't always punished.

I have spoken so far about two dangers faced by publishing today: first, publishers self-censoring their own ideas, and second, the ill-considered initiatives of managers who know too little about the objects they are dealing with (the books themselves). But there's a further danger, which is there for everyone to see: the campaign against copyright.

In this campaign, now in full swing, there are hidden motives that go well beyond the sphere of authors' rights. The secret motivation behind this movement is a disdain for what Italian law describes as "creative work." The refusal to remunerate it, in a civilization that makes it illegal not to pay cleaning staff, implies that creative work is not to be regarded as actual work. But, if it isn't this, then how should it be considered? As publicity by the author for himself, where payment for the publicity is made in kind—and this would be the labor itself carried out by the author in giving form to his work. If we accept this point of view, the author wouldn't live on the profits derived from the sale of his work, but on the fact that his work has produced invitations to public events, commissions, consultancies, summer schools, which will have to be adequately remunerated. And this would reestablish a tolerable balance.

For such an idea to filter into public opinion and eventually establish itself, as in fact it has, every type of work has to be regarded as *communication*: a formless concept, with neither beginning nor end, involving people who count much the same as subjects in a statistical sample. This shameful and depressing situation corresponds with the *forced esotericism* that is an ever more apparent characteristic of the unnameable present. In the same way that in the *sattras*—the boldest, ultimate, and interminable Vedic rites—the distinction between the sacrificer and the officiants disappeared, and with it the obligation to pay ritual fees (*dakṣiṇā*, without which the rite itself could not be regarded as effective), so too in the Internet world there is a tendency to reduce the distinction between work and communication, between author and generic keyboard user. Consequently there will also be no obligation to remunerate the work of the author, since everyone is an author. Some of the most vociferous opinion makers of today regard this state of affairs as a victory for democracy, a global democracy that will be a prelude to other victories to be achieved not just on the Web. And this is a more subtle and up-to-date form of the *bêtise* that scourged the world in the times of Baudelaire and Flaubert. But equipped obviously with much greater means—as well as a ubiquitous potential.

Having said this, I wouldn't wish to give the impression that publishing today, in the sense I have attempted to describe—namely publishing where the publisher is happy only if he succeeds in publishing good books—is a lost cause. It is, instead, simply a very tough cause. But no tougher than it was in 1499, when Aldus Manutius of

Venice published a novel by an unknown author, written in a composite language consisting of Italian, Latin, and Greek. Its format was also unusual, as were the many woodcuts that studded the text. And yet it is the most beautiful book printed up to now: the *Hypnerotomachia Poliphili*. Someone could still attempt sometime to equal it.

Textual Note

The writings that make up this book are all linked to some particular occasion, as is clearly apparent. I hope this is not viewed negatively, even though I am well aware that the names of Aldus Manutius and Kurt Wolff appear rather too often. But a large part of publishing life is entrusted to the oral tradition, with rare incursions into the written word, so that certain set passages are bound to reappear each time, without which the argument lacks support. Moreover, it is never a good idea to take certain things for granted if it is true in this respect, and in other instances, that the memory tends to shrink as more and more information becomes available. The list below indicates where the pieces in this book first appeared or were first read.

I

Publishing as a Literary Genre: Conference held at the Ščusev State Museum of Architecture, Moscow, on October 17, 2001.

II

Singular Books: The first part (pp. 17–31) appeared in *La Repubblica* on December 27–28, 2006; the second part (pp. 31–71) was previously unpublished; the third part (pp. 71–79) was delivered at the opening of the exhibition *Religions and Mythologies: A Journey Through the Adelphi Catalog,* January 24, 1995, at the Biblioteca dei Frati in Lugano.

A Letter to a Stranger: Preface to *Cento lettere a uno sconosciuto* (Milan: Adelphi, 2003).

III

Giulio Einaudi: Appeared in *Il Corriere della Sera*, April 15, 1999.

Luciano Foà: Appeared in *La Repubblica*, January 29, 2005.

Roger Straus: Published in *Roger W. Straus: A Celebration* (New York: Farrar, Straus and Giroux, 2005), pp. 115–18.

Peter Suhrkamp: Appeared in *Il Corriere della Sera*, October 19, 1975.

Vladimir Dimitrijević: Speech given in Lausanne to mark the twentieth anniversary of Éditions L'Âge d'Homme, November 6, 1986.

IV

Faire Plaisir: Unpublished text.

The Obliteration of Publisher Identity: Speech given in Paris during the proceedings of the Bureau International de l'Édition Française, December 1, 2011.

Aldus Manutius's Fly Sheet: Speech given at the Fòrum Atlàntida, "La funció social de l'editor," Barcelona, November 3, 2009.